Populations and Precarity during the COVID-19 Pandemic

The **ISEAS – Yusof Ishak Institute** (formerly Institute of Southeast Asian Studies) is an autonomous organization established in 1968. It is a regional centre dedicated to the study of socio-political, security, and economic trends and developments in Southeast Asia and its wider geostrategic and economic environment. The Institute's research programmes are grouped under Regional Economic Studies (RES), Regional Strategic and Political Studies (RSPS), and Regional Social and Cultural Studies (RSCS). The Institute is also home to the ASEAN Studies Centre (ASC), the Singapore APEC Study Centre, and the Temasek History Research Centre (THRC).

ISEAS Publishing, an established academic press, has issued more than 2,000 books and journals. It is the largest scholarly publisher of research about Southeast Asia from within the region. ISEAS Publishing works with many other academic and trade publishers and distributors to disseminate important research and analyses from and about Southeast Asia to the rest of the world.

Populations and Precarity during the COVID-19 Pandemic

Southeast Asian Perspectives

Edited by
Kevin S.Y. Tan • Steve K.L. Chan

First published in Singapore in 2023 by
ISEAS Publishing
30 Heng Mui Keng Terrace
Singapore 119614

E-mail: publish@iseas.edu.sg
Website: <http://bookshop.iseas.edu.sg>

All rights reserved. No part of this publication may be reproduced, stored in a retrieval system, or transmitted in any form or by any means, electronic, mechanical, photocopying, recording or otherwise, without the prior permission of the ISEAS – Yusof Ishak Institute.

© 2023 ISEAS – Yusof Ishak Institute, Singapore

The responsibility for facts and opinions in this publication rests exclusively with the authors and their interpretations do not necessarily reflect the views or the policy of the publisher or its supporters.

ISEAS Library Cataloguing-in-Publication Data

Name(s): Tan, Kevin S.Y., editor. | Chan, Steve K.L., editor.
Title: Populations and precarity during the COVID-19 pandemic: Southeast Asian perspectives / edited by Kevin S.Y. Tan and Steve K.L. Chan.
Description: Singapore : ISEAS-Yusof Ishak Institute, 2023. | Includes bibliographical references and index.
Identifiers: ISBN 978-981-4881-29-6 (soft cover) | ISBN 978-981-4951-50-0 (e-book PDF) | ISBN 978-981-4951-53-1 (epub)
Subjects: LCSH: Southeast Asia—Social conditions. | COVID-19 Pandemic, 2020—Social aspects—Southeast Asia. | Southeast Asia—Population.
Classification: LCC HB3641 P83

Cover design by Lee Meng Hui
Index compiled by Sheryl Sin Bing Peng
Typesetting by International Typesetters Pte Ltd
Printed in Singapore by Mainland Press Pte Ltd

CONTENTS

Preface   vii

About the Contributors   ix

1. Introduction: Populations, Precarity and the COVID-19 Pandemic
   Kevin S.Y. Tan and Steve K.L. Chan   1

2. Transformation of the Family Structure in Southeast Asia: Trends and Implications
   Premchand Dommaraju   12

3. New Normal, Old Ties: COVID-19's Social Impact on the Singapore-Johor Bahru Connection
   Kevin S.Y. Tan and Grace Lim   28

4. Unequal Flows: Examining the Factors Surrounding Thai and Vietnamese Labour Migration to South Korea
   Steve K.L. Chan   50

5. Emplacing Multiculturalism: Southeast Asian Migrant Linguistic Acculturation Programmes and Community Building in South Korea
   Ivan V. Small   68

6.	"Foreign Talent" in Singapore and Some Implications for Schools *Jason Tan and Lana Khong*	84
7.	Managing Disaster Risk and Enabling Social Protection in Thailand: Some Lessons from the COVID-19 Pandemic *Prapaporn Tivayanond Mongkhonvanit*	101
8.	Transnational Housing Insecurity: Mobility, Homelessness, and the COVID-19 Pandemic *Kok-Hoe Ng and Jeyda Simren Sekhon Atac*	120
9.	Older Persons with Hearing Disabilities in Indonesia: Vulnerability and Demographic Diversity during the COVID-19 Pandemic *Evi Nurvidya Arifin, Chang-Yau Hoon and Aris Ananta*	144

Index   167

PREFACE

The origins of this edited volume stem from a two-day online webinar series on *Managing Demographic Change in Southeast Asia: Challenges and Issues amidst the 'New Normal'*, which was held from 19–20 November 2020 and hosted by the ISEAS – Yusof Ishak Institute.

At that time, the COVID-19 coronavirus had already spread throughout many parts of the world, and the situation declared a pandemic. It was something that many people had not experienced before, especially its wide-reaching global nature. Few communities, if any, were spared the impact of the pandemic. Within the span of a year, the pandemic not only claimed thousands of lives, but also closed international borders, disrupted air travel between countries and devastated the livelihood of countless others in societies all around the world.

The abovementioned workshop, therefore, not only provided a timely and important platform for a dialogue on the complex and multifaceted demographic issues emerging across Southeast Asia, but also connected them to the challenges of the COVID-19 pandemic on various communities and the lived experiences of many persons living in the region.

By 2022, however, it seems that the pandemic has been gradually receding. With increasing numbers of persons having been vaccinated against the COVID-19 coronavirus, many countries are gradually reopening with the resumption of international travel. Although there is more progress to be made in the fight against the pandemic, there has been a growing but cautious sense of hope that perhaps the worst is over. Many countries in Southeast Asia have reopened their borders with the recognition that the virus is considered "endemic" as part of a broader narrative of the "new normal" in a post-COVID-19 world.

This edited volume is, then, an important scholarly response to discussing the outcomes and potential futures that will result from such a "new normal". Combining selected papers from the abovementioned webinar series, along with invited authors, a key theme that has emerged is the concept of precarity and its relationship with various populations throughout Southeast Asia. With the ongoing realities of social inequality and cultural diversity that many societies face, the COVID-19 pandemic has exacerbated the uncertainties that many encounter in all aspects of everyday life. Consequently, we hope that this collection will provide insightful perspectives to enable a deeper appreciation of such challenges and lead to potential efforts to overcome them.

Kevin S.Y. Tan and Steve K.L. Chan
The Editors

ABOUT THE CONTRIBUTORS

Kevin S.Y. Tan is a sociologist and cultural anthropologist. He is a Lecturer at the Chua Thian Poh Community Leadership Centre at the National University of Singapore. His research interests include borderlands studies, transnational migrant flows, urban enclaves and street-level informal economies such as night markets and bazaars.

Grace Lim holds a degree in Economics and Management from the University of London International Programmes. She is currently a Cyber Threat Intelligence Consultant, analyzing the intersection of Geopolitics and Cybersecurity. As an independent researcher, her research interest lies in the area of Global Security and Mobility.

Steve K.L. Chan is an Assistant Professor of Sociology at the Keimyung University, South Korea. He has been affiliated with the Social Research Institute of Chulalongkorn University and the Regional Center for Social Science and Sustainable Development of the Chiangmai University as Visiting Research Fellow.

Ivan V. Small is Associate Professor of Anthropology at the University of Houston. He is author of *Currencies of Imagination: Channeling Money and Chasing Mobility in Vietnam* (2019), co-editor of *Money at the Margins: Global Perspectives on Technology, Financial Inclusion and Design* (2018), and has published numerous articles, chapters and op-eds on Vietnam's migration and remittance patterns, economic transitions and transnational connections. He has held fellowships at the Institute for Money, Technology and Financial Inclusion at the University of California Irvine and the ISEAS – Yusof Ishak Institute in Singapore, among others. He was previously a Fulbright-Hays visiting scholar at Vietnam National University, and holds a PhD from Cornell University.

Jason Tan is Associate Professor in Policy, Curriculum & Leadership at the National Institute of Education. Among his latest publications is *Teacher Preparation in Singapore: A Concise Critical History* (co-authored with Yeow-Tong Chia and Alistair Chew, 2022).

Lana Khong is a part-time Lecturer in Policy, Curriculum & Leadership at the National Institute of Education. She thoroughly enjoys facilitating the teaching and learning of new and experienced educators who grapple with diverse challenges in the ever-changing social and education landscape. Currently, she is also actively involved in leadership development and life coaching in a variety of contexts.

Premchand Dommaraju is Associate Professor of Sociology and Director of the MSc in Applied Gerontology programme at Nanyang Technological University, Singapore. His research focuses on socio-demographic issues related to marriage, families, and households, and ageing in Southeast and South Asia focusing on the common demographic issues faced by the diverse societies in the two regions. His works have appeared in leading demographic journals including *Population and Development Review*, *Demographic Research*, *Population*, and *Population Studies*.

Prapaporn Tivayanond Mongkhonvanit is the Dean of the School of Global Studies at Thammasat University. She was a Board Member of the National Council on Social Welfare of Thailand and the Founding Director of Social Policy and Development (SPD) International Programme at Thammasat University. Prapaporn is currently leading the SDG Lab at the School of Global Studies, and is working on promoting a vital connection between localization and globalization under the SDGs. Her research and publications cover social protection & welfare, social entrepreneurship, and social policy innovation.

About the Contributors

Kok-Hoe Ng is a Senior Research Fellow and Head of the Social Inclusion Project at the Lee Kuan Yew School of Public Policy, National University of Singapore. He is a social policy researcher whose work focuses on housing and income security. He led Singapore's first nationwide street count of homelessness and founded the Social Inclusion Project at the Lee Kuan Yew School of Public Policy. Among his latest publications is *They told us to move: Dakota—Cassia* (co-editor, 2019).

Jeyda Simren Sekhon Atac is a Research Assistant in the Social Inclusion Project at the Lee Kuan Yew School of Public Policy, National University of Singapore. She completed her Masters in Comparative and International Education at the University of Oxford, during which she was a Leading for Impact Fellow. She also volunteers widely, both in Singapore and remotely, with initiatives working to create social impact internationally.

Evi Nurvidya Arifin is a Senior Assistant Professor at the Centre for Advanced Research (CARe), Universiti Brunei Darussalam and Adjunct Researcher at the Demographic Institute, Faculty of Economics and Business, Universitas Indonesia, Indonesia. She did her postdoctoral fellowship at Asian MetaCentre for Population and Sustainable Development Analysis, and Asia Research Institute, National University of Singapore. She was a Visiting Research Fellow at the Institute of Southeast Asian Studies (now called the ISEAS – Yusof Ishak Institute). Her research interests cover disability, population ageing, migration, and poverty.

Chang-Yau Hoon is a Professor at the Institute of Asian Studies, Universiti Brunei Darussalam, and also an Adjunct Research Fellow at the University of Western Australia. He was the Director of the Centre for Advanced Research at UBD from July 2017 to June 2022. He specializes in Chinese diaspora, identity politics, multiculturalism, and religious and cultural diversity in contemporary Southeast Asia.

Aris Ananta is a Professor at the Faculty of Economics and Business, Universitas Indonesia; Visiting Professor at the Centre for Advanced

Research (CARe), Universiti Brunei Darussalam; and Adjunct Researcher at Demographic Institute, Faculty of Economics and Business, Universitas Indonesia. He was President of Asia Population Association (2019–21); Senior Research Fellow at the Institute of Southeast Asian Studies during 2001–14; and Senior Fellow at Department of Economics, National University of Singapore in 1999–2000. His research interests include ageing population, population mobility, social protection, poverty, and ethnicity. His regional research interest includes Indonesia, Brunei, Southeast Asia, and Asia.

1

INTRODUCTION: POPULATIONS, PRECARITY AND THE COVID-19 PANDEMIC

Kevin S.Y. Tan and Steve K.L. Chan

THE COVID-19 PANDEMIC AND ITS IMPACT

The outbreak of the COVID-19 coronavirus from late 2019 transformed, in many ways, the order of many things in our lives. This pandemic was a major global health challenge in the twenty-first century that has so far been unrivalled in scale and impact. Many lives were lost during the first two years due to its potentially dangerous effects on the human body, particularly among the physically and economically vulnerable. Although Southeast Asia had encountered earlier epidemics such as SARS[1] and MERS[2] in previous years, nothing quite prepared the countries in this region for the social and economic fallout that resulted from not just the disease, but also its corresponding effects on the infrastructural aspects of a country. This included the healthcare system, the education system, the transport system, entertainment industries, and even the capacity for residents of a country to access public spaces. Dubbed a "new normal", such a challenging experience obviously changed the lives of many in various societies throughout Southeast Asia. Apart from the tragedy of those who succumbed to the pandemic, the ones who survived it will likely carry the burden of coming to terms with its consequences and the changes it has incorporated into everyday living.

Many will recall that during its initial months, governments around the world and even the media tended to regard it as an epidemic that was largely limited to a single country, China. Although it was in China where most researchers today would admit where the COVID-19 coronavirus first emerged, it was presumed that sealing the country's borders might contain the situation. Alarmingly, waves of outbreaks spread in varying intensity around the globe. Its rapid spread in a matter of months to almost every continent via a global network of travel and migration appeared to be inevitable. In the case of South Korea, for example, the city of Daegu recorded a cluster infection in a local church, starting a string of transmissions that would spin out of control. While the traditional approach of testing and contact tracing had initially worked well (Kim 2020), the scale of infection eventually spread everywhere. Finally, it became apparent that the COVID-19 coronavirus would become a full-blown pandemic that would exceed the severity of SARS and MERS, exhibiting similar characteristics to the influenza pandemic of 1918 also known as the 'Spanish Flu'.

Following growing self-consciousness of its spread and dangers, health authorities in every country began to announce infection and death rates daily. Statistics of infectious diseases had never been so closely followed around the world until the COVID-19 pandemic. There was a prevailing sense of fear and impending doom in many countries around the world, but this was also interestingly, and perhaps unfortunately, contradicted by misinformed scepticism and rejection of the epidemiological reality of this pandemic. Many communities were divided, particularly in Western countries, on whether the safety measures put in place by governments were acceptable or, on the other hand for others, even sufficient. In the midst of the panic buying of food, medical face masks, antiseptic hand wash and other daily necessities resulted in images of empty shelves in stores and supermarkets, as thousands gradually fell victim to its deadly symptoms.

While most of the countries of Southeast Asia appeared to show a measure of resilience in the early months of 2020, this was eventually overtaken by surges in infections that saw even well-policed societies like Singapore failing to hold back infections, particularly among its migrant worker dormitories.

It was natural, then, that much was expected of governments around the world in responding to the growing infection numbers. Many countries in Southeast Asia adopted a two-pronged policy approach. The first approach was to curb the spread of the disease, which was followed by attempts to rescue or minimize its impact on the local economy, while enabling protection for the most vulnerable and the unemployed. Public health measures employed were enforced with a combination of lockdown and curfew, with social distancing measures. Throughout the rest of 2020, international borders were indefinitely closed, along with restrictions on domestic travel. This greatly affected tourism, migration and the airline industry, resulting in often-irreparable huge losses. At the same time, some governments strengthened their welfare programmes and reinforced unemployment benefits to relieve sectors hit hard by the pandemic, either directly or indirectly, such as the entertainment business involving nightlife where large crowds would often gather. Wealthier first-world nations pushed out economic stimulation packages without the need for means testing.

LIFE UNDER PANDEMIC LOCKDOWNS

Many would recall that it was only by the end of 2020 where viable vaccines were made widely available to the world, although the initial months that followed revealed global inequalities in terms of access. Nevertheless, until the emergence of vaccines, the only way for governments to slow COVID-19 coronavirus transmissions and to "flatten the curve" had been to introduce social distancing protocols. The World Health Organization (WHO) (2020) distinguished these into four categories, namely: personal measures, physical and social distancing measures, movement measures and special protection measures. Personal measures were mainly about personal hygiene and wearing a mask in public venues. Distancing measures during the pandemic mandated that people should maintain between one and three metres away from each other, depending on varying authorities. Due to such measures, the number of persons allowed at certain venues like schools, restaurants and cinemas were highly restricted. This subsequently reduced business hours, often leading to their eventual shutdown.

The social distancing measures banned or restricted individuals from travelling locally or internationally, except for essential or extraordinary reasons. In particular, special attention was directed to what were considered more vulnerable groups such as seniors and persons with underlying medical conditions. Furthermore, with the onset of periodic waves of infection in various countries in Southeast Asia, it was often revealed that the greatest victims of the pandemic have been low-income transient migrant workers, ethnic minorities and those living under squalid conditions in deprived areas where infections tended to grow uncontrollably (Lauvrak and Juvet 2020). Lockdowns often rendered them literally trapped in their living quarters, not to mention having limited access to local health care, especially for undocumented workers. Upon being treated, many displayed severe symptoms due to delayed access to medical treatment. Consequently, these communities suffered both physically and psychologically. This was usually compounded by xenophobia from the host society, as well as income insecurity that came about due to workplace closures or job losses (Guadagno 2020).

At the same time, while adopting a global and transnational perspective, it is informative to recall that the pandemic not only affected migrant workers but also their families in their country of origin, which are often developing societies. This is because many families of migrant workers rely on their regular remittances to overcome the costs of living (Takenaka et al. 2020). A central and recurring theme that resonates in the experiences of such communities has been their vulnerability to the unpredictable nature of the pandemic at the height of its spread. However, this is not to imply that other groups in a COVID-19 world faced lesser dangers. This recognition of precarity, as experienced by members of a precariat (Standing 2014) in every country, should also extend to the fact that some of the most vulnerable persons to the dangers posed by the pandemic were the frontline medical workers involving first-responders, nurses and doctors. This is because the entire public health system risks collapse if infections were to also severely incapacitate the role of health workers.

OVERVIEW OF THE CHAPTERS IN THIS VOLUME

The origins of this collection of chapters stem from a series of scholarly presentations from a two-day conference titled "Managing Demographic Change in Southeast Asia: Challenges and Issues amidst the 'New Normal'" that ran from 20–21 November 2020. As part of the "new normal", the event was entirely hosted online by the ISEAS – Yusof Ishak Institute[3], and supported by Konrad-Adenauer-Stiftung, a German political foundation dedicated to the promotion of liberal democracy and a social market economy. At the time of writing, with the pandemic evolving into an endemic reality for many societies in both Southeast Asia and beyond, this book is a reflection of its impact and ensuing consequences. The issues and questions evoked from various presentations at the conference, together with other additional authors invited for this collection, remain important arenas for scholarly discussion during this challenging period. Combined with an awareness of the pandemic, the perspectives of each contributor of this volume enable a useful platform in engaging a range of topics, particularly in the areas of mobility, migration, transnationalism and social marginality in the face of ongoing demographic trends that shape Southeast Asia.

Taken as a whole, the range of issues raised by the various authors may be seen as a mutual attempt at addressing and making sense of various social-cultural and economic issues while relating them to the broader narrative of precarity shaped by the COVID-19 coronavirus pandemic. Nothing, therefore, brings to the fore, our existential vulnerability as quickly as a potentially deadly disease that will not distinguish between culture, religion, nationality, gender or social class. In other words, this collection seeks to examine the various policy implications of this recent pandemic together with the precariousness of our lived experiences by not merely focusing on the pandemic itself in terms of infection counts or death tolls, but by revealing its capacity to disrupt key areas of everyday life within communities with strong ties to the region.

As a multi-ethnic and diverse region, Southeast Asia consists of countries experiencing various levels of development and demographic shifts. Amidst such diversity, there will be persons and certain communities that will be more vulnerable in view of their social, cultural, economic or embodied precarity. Consequently, it is already a challenge for them to negotiate the necessities and regular needs of daily events, let alone in times of adverse situations, such as natural disasters or in this case, a pandemic. Such precarity often emerges from a lack of capacity to deal with even the most "ordinary" of affairs in the face of a sudden and unexpected loss of income or health. Recovery is also often a long-drawn and difficult process that could lead to a worsening of one's situation if adequate support or stability is not given in a timely manner. Hence, the experience of migrants as part of "low-end" globalization (Mathews 2011) have been some of the most affected by the pandemic due to their socially marginal and disempowered status as mentioned earlier. As international borders were hastily closed in order to minimize the spread of the infection (Nouvellet et al. 2021), such migrants were often trapped in their places of employment and also remained far from their home countries. Unfortunately, such communities of migrants have often been conveniently scapegoated as potential spreaders of infectious disease (Ullah et al. 2021) under conditions that were not of their making.

The chapters in this volume, therefore, adopt approaches reflecting a range of academic fields that include education, anthropology, sociology, demography, migration studies, disability studies, development studies and social policy analysis. More specifically, the following eight chapters of this volume address issues related to ageing, inequality, migration, diversity, housing and employment in connection with a pandemic-ridden Southeast Asia. In Chapter 2, we start with Dommaraju's discussion of how the family structure has changed due to demographic shifts in recent decades. He broadly explores the demographic trends in Southeast Asia, which remains a critical platform to understand how population changes also impact the experience of the pandemic and vice versa. The pandemic's full impact on processes such as fertility, mortality, life expectancy and migration are only becoming more apparent as COVID-19 infections recede in various parts of the world. While not directly addressing the pandemic directly, Dommaraju very importantly lays the demographic foundation and context in relation to subsequent chapters that are fundamentally tied to the issue of population flows within and beyond Southeast Asia.

It is useful, then, to recall that the countries in the region are at different stages of demographic transition, with some having an expanding younger population while others experiencing rapid ageing.

For example, later marriage and the later outward migration by young adults are common for certain younger societies. However, for ageing societies, there are further implications for family support, social welfare and labour market issues. These concerns are addressed from different vantage points in Chapters 3 to 5. Tan and Lim's (Chapter 3) reflections on the Singapore-Johor Bahru Connection; Chan's (Chapter 4) examination of Thai and Vietnamese migrant workers to South Korea; and Small's (Chapter 5) insights derived from the linguistic acculturation programmes of migrants in South Korea further contextualize the challenges of migration and cross-border issues. At the same time, they underline the importance of how Southeast Asia should be understood as an interconnected region within and beyond it. In spite of the border lockdowns during the pandemic and tight restrictions to international travel, such networks remain but have been, admittedly, strained and transformed.

In Chapter 3, Tan and Lim reflect on the impact of the border lockdown between Singapore and Malaysia because of the pandemic. It effectively prevented, for each side respectively, much needed migrant labour from Malaysia and monetary flows from Singapore in the form of short-term tourism, among other consequences. This resulted in challenges for Singapore's labour infrastructure while it devastated the economic growth of Johor Bahru, the Malaysian city just across the border. Simultaneously, this chapter seeks to recall the social and emotional costs of such a prolonged separation. It is argued that such lockdowns are seldom sustainable because the social-cultural spaces between Singapore and Johor Bahru have become an integral part of the everyday lives of thousands of persons on both sides of the border, due to the intense nature of transborder mobilities. In the face of future border lockdowns of a similar nature, a more nuanced response by both the Singaporean and Malaysian governments in managing this longstanding relationship should be considered.

In Chapter 4, Chan examines the migrant trends of Vietnamese and Thai migrant workers in South Korea. He proposes a model of "unequal flows" regarding unskilled labour that is influenced by factors such as population ageing and labour migration patterns. Although migrant workers in South Korea had been adversely affected during the lockdown, a "reverse flow" emerged rapidly by mid-2022 as populations in both the labour sending and receiving countries became vaccinated against the COVID-19 coronavirus. Consequently, Vietnam's desire for labour due to post-pandemic globalization drew Vietnamese workers back home to fill job vacancies. Also based in South Korea, Small's insights in Chapter 5 examined its growing multicultural society that is seeing an increased number of migrant brides from Vietnam, which is also complicated by the COVID-19 pandemic. Pre-departure training-upon-arrival linguistic acculturation programmes are offered to facilitate the integration of these new migrants. There is also local support for these multicultural families, which more than often consists of a marriage between a Korean husband and a Vietnamese wife. More importantly, Korean "multiculturalism" could be better understood as a bilateral policy where South Korea's "New Southern Policy" encourages its industries to invest and relocate their production plants to Southeast Asia, in particular, Vietnam.

The next two chapters provide a structural perspective on how population flows and demographic shifts in the areas of education and social protection relate to potential complications that accompany a sense of precarity. More specifically, they relate to tensions in national integration for a relatively young nation and the experience of managing natural disasters in a developing country. This is discussed in policies addressing foreign-local stakeholder dynamics (Tan and Khong in Chapter 6) and the evolution of social protection policies informed by the challenges of the COVID-19 pandemic (Prapaporn in Chapter 7). Tan and Khong's analysis of "Foreign Talent" policies in Singapore's education system offers a nuanced understanding of how the conscious inclusion of foreign-born teaching professionals and students into the island-state's education system in recent years appears to be less stable than it may appear. They identify a key source of such potential instability to competitive dynamics emerging from the "replacement migration" of ethnically-similar but culturally-distinct people groups into an environment that is still ambivalent regarding what constitutes a "Singapore core". What is suggested by Tan and Khong is the need for greater reciprocity in such efforts, and even more so in a time of challenges towards the delivery of education amidst unprecedented pedagogical practices, such as the use of "home-based learning" through online mediums.

Moving from Singapore to Thailand, Mongkhonvanit's "Managing Disaster Risk in Thailand" in Chapter 7, highlights the systemic policy lessons learnt in implementing various programmes to reduce the risks and relieve the impacts of natural disasters. Although Thailand has undergone vast leaps in economic development in recent decades, its level of social inequality remains high, thus exacerbating the precarity of the less privileged. As a response to the outbreak of the COVID-19 coronavirus, the Thai authorities offered emergency social protection measures in the form of cash assistance for informal sector workers and farmers, for example. However, institutional frameworks limit social protection programmes by being less integrated with local disaster risk management policies. Existing social security schemes for poor individuals, families and children, therefore, should be expanded to cater for increasing needs arising during the lockdowns, associated employment loss and subsequent economic downturn. More policy changes are recommended to facilitate the application of more *proactive* than *reactive* approaches that will add to a more resilient support system to those who have fallen beyond any conventional social-economic safety nets in place.

The final two chapters adopt a more grounded view on the experience of precarity—the hearing impaired and the homeless, or more specifically, those facing transnational housing insecurity. Both of these groups encountered daily challenges that were significantly worsened by the arrival of the COVID-19 pandemic. Noting that mostly of those facing housing insecurity were from single-person and male households, Ng and Sekhon Atac's (Chapter 8) original and well-documented study of Singaporean migrants in Malaysia and Indonesia clearly suggests that precarity can occur even among citizens of high-GDP and relatively affluent societies like Singapore. Many of their respondents have been stuck in Singapore during pandemic-related border closures, putting them in a *de facto* state of homelessness. Having adopted transnational living that entails transient stays in Malaysia and Indonesia, such Singaporeans are now facing social, economic and institutional dislocation due to the COVID-19 pandemic. At the same time, their choices in assuming such a lifestyle also have correlations with broader demographic shifts in Singapore.

Finally, to complement the previous chapter's recognition of spatial precarity in terms of housing insecurity, Arifin, Hoon and Ananta's contribution (Chapter 9) complete this volume by investigating how older persons with hearing disabilities in Indonesia traverse the challenges of their embodied precarity. They argue that the pandemic has exacted a double toll on their disadvantaged status by worsening hearing capability. Some reasons for this lie in the ironic impact of pandemic safety measures such as the wearing of face masks to reduce the chances of infection, which also impedes the capacity for lip reading, effectively reducing an important mode of communication for the hearing impaired. This has also inadvertently reduced the chances for securing stable employment, revealing just how even the smallest of changes or restrictions to our everyday practices can have large and lasting consequences.

Admittedly, while we concede that this volume of chapters will not be able to provide a fully comprehensive discussion on the link between population flows and its relation to social and economic precarity, we hope that it will at least begin to address some of them. Neither will it answer all the problems emerging or eventually worsened by the "new normal" of the COVID-19 pandemic. However, in the wake of a challenging two-and-half year duration since the start of this global wave of suffering and death for many, perhaps a way to recover from it is to learn and subsequently grow stronger and wiser in its wake.

NOTES

1. SARS - Severe acute respiratory syndrome
2. MERS - Middle East Respiratory Syndrome
3. Previously the Institute of Southeast Asian Studies

REFERENCES

Guadagno, Lorenzo. 2020. *Migrants and the COVID-19 Pandemic: An Initial Analysis*. Geneva, Switzerland: International Organization for Migration. https://reliefweb.int/report/world/migrants-and-covid-19-pandemic-initial-analysis.

Kim, June-Ho, Julia Ah-Reum An, Pok-kee Min, Asaf Bitton, and Atul A. Gawande. 2020. "How South Korea Responded to the Covid-19 Outbreak in Daegu". *NEJM Catalyst Innovations in Care Delivery* 1, no. 4. https://doi.org/10.1056/CAT.20.0159.

Lauvrak, Vigdis and Lene Juvet. 2020. *COVID-19 Epidemic: Social and Economic Vulnerable Groups during the COVID-19 Pandemic–a Rapid Review*. Norwegian Institute of Public Health.

Mathews, Gordon. 2011. *Ghetto at the Centre of the World*. Chicago and London: University of Chicago Press.

Nouvellet, Pierre et al. 2021. "Reduction in Mobility and COVID-19 Transmission". *Nature Communications* 12: 1090. https://doi.org/10.1038/s41467-021-21358-2.

Standing, Guy. 2014. *The Precariat: The New Dangerous Class*. London and New York: Bloomsbury Academic.

Takenaka, Aiko Kikkawa, Raymond Gaspar, James Villafuerte, and Badri Narayanan. 2020. "COVID-19 Impact on International Migration, Remittances, and Recipient Households in Developing Asia". *ADB Brief* 148 (August). Manila: Asia Development Bank. http://dx.doi.org/10.22617/BRF200219-2.

Ullah, Akm Ahsan, Faraha Nawaz, and Diotima Chattoraj. 2021. "Locked up under Lockdown: The COVID-19 Pandemic and the Migrant Population". *Social Sciences & Humanities Open* 3, no. 1: 100126. https://doi.org/10.1016/j.ssaho.2021.100126.

World Health Organization. 2020. "Overview of Public Health and Social Measures in the Context of COVID-19: Interim Guidance", 18 May 2020. https://www.who.int/publications/i/item/overview-of-public-health-and-social-measures-in-the-context-of-covid-19.

2

TRANSFORMATION OF THE FAMILY STRUCTURE IN SOUTHEAST ASIA: TRENDS AND IMPLICATIONS

Premchand Dommaraju

INTRODUCTION

All three demographic components—births, migration, and mortality—influence multiple aspects of families and households. Southeast Asia has witnessed substantial demographic changes notable of which are steep declines in fertility, increase in both intra-regional and international migration, and considerable lengthening of life expectancy. While the family continues to be a central institution, many aspects of the family are changing. Demographic literature on the causes and consequences of family change in the region is limited. At a more fundamental level, what constitutes a family during times of demographic change, as observed by Farris (2020, p. 4) in a different context, needs to be redefined to "include any group of people who are unified, cooperative, and care for each other".

Using census and survey data from seven countries in the region and reviewing demographic reports between 1980 and 2017, this chapter examines demographic changes and their linkages to transformations in the family structure in the region. The chapter highlights the changes in family structure resulting from later marriage, greater marital instability, delay in young people leaving home, and a growing number of older persons.

DEMOGRAPHIC CHANGES IN SOUTHEAST ASIA

Changes in births, migration, and life expectancy are discussed first. This is followed by an extended discussion of changes in marriage. Although marriage is not a formal demographic component (as it cannot directly alter population size or structure), it is closely tied to births in the region. Most births in the region occur within marriage, and the institution of marriage has not lost its relevance.

Declining number of children. In just over three decades, the average fertility rate has declined from more than five to replacement levels in most of the region (United Nations 2019b). Even in countries with relatively higher fertility, such as the Philippines, fertility has been declining though at a gradual pace. The declines have been attributed to various factors from the success of family planning programmes to economic development. One key reason for the decline is the impressive expansion of education, especially for girls, which has led to delays in marriage and brought about ideational changes regarding family sizes (Hull 2012).

International migration has grown in importance. The number of international migrants from the region doubled between 2000 and 2015, with about 70 per cent moving within the region (Tey 2017). International migrants constitute more than 10 per cent of the population in Singapore and Malaysia (Tey 2017). The countries in the region serve as both destination and sending countries. The main emigrant sending nations include the Philippines, Indonesia, and Myanmar, with nearly 23.6 million emigrants from the region (IOM 2021). Much of the migration is fuelled by economic factors, but there is a growing number for family reasons such as transnational marriage. In addition to international migration, the region has significant flows within countries primarily from rural to urban areas. The share of the population living in urban areas in the region increased from about one-quarter in 1980 to close to one-half by 2017 (United Nations 2018). Rural to urban migration is predominated by young migrants. In the largest cities in the region, including Jakarta, Bangkok, and Manila, there are more female migrants, attracted by employment opportunities in manufacturing, service, and domestic sectors (Jones and Dommaraju 2012).

Increasing life expectancy across the region. Life expectancy has lengthened in the region due to reductions in child and adult mortality rates. These declines mean that two-thirds of children born can expect to survive to age 65 (Basten 2015). Apart from Lao and Myanmar, life expectancy in the region is close to or above 70 years. As a result of mortality transition and fertility declines, the number and share of older people in the population are set to increase. By 2050 there will be close to 150 million people older than 65 in the region; the number of older people in the region will exceed those aged 0 to 14, and the number of deaths will exceed births quite soon after that by 2060 (United Nations 2019b). Some countries in the region will experience a rapid rate of ageing—Thailand will double its share of older population in just 22 years compared to more than 70 years it took for countries such as Australia and Sweden (UNESCAP 2017).

Men and women are in increasing numbers delaying marriage, and some are foregoing marriage. Early marriages have fallen, with the proportion of girls married before age 18 declining throughout the region. In Indonesia, for instance, the proportion married in the age group 15–19 dropped from 38 per cent in 1971 to 9 per cent by 2015 (United Nations 2019a; Badan Pusat Statistik 2015). While marriage is delayed at younger ages, most men and women who marry will marry in their mid to late 20s, with median age of less than 25 (see Figure 2.1). However, there are large variations within countries such as Thailand and the Philippines.

A notable exception is the increasing number of women who will never marry in their lifetime. In Singapore, Thailand, and Myanmar, between 20 and 25 per cent of women aged 30–34 were never married, and a significant proportion of them will never marry in their lifetime (Yeung and Hu 2018). In these countries, non-marriage is a growing trend. In Thailand, the proportion of never-married women aged 30–34 tripled from 8 per cent in 1970 to 22 per cent by 2015 (United Nations 2019a). As elsewhere in Asia, key driving forces of these changes in the region include educational expansion for girls, ideational and normative changes, and economic transformations (Jones and Yeung 2014).

Transnational marriages and cohabitation. Transnational marriages constitute an increasingly larger share of marriages in several countries in the region. Almost 40 per cent of marriages in Singapore involve a spouse who is not a Singapore citizen (Yeung and Hu 2018). Several countries in the region serve as sending countries for marriage

FIGURE 2.1
Women's Marriage Age in Southeast Asia

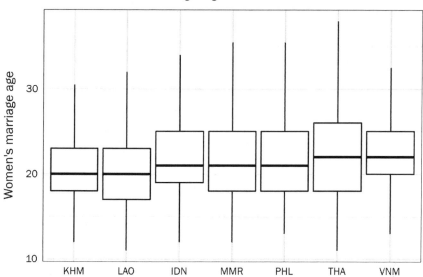

Notes: Cambodia 2014 (KHM), Laos 2017 (LAO), Indonesia 2017 (IDN), Myanmar 2015–16 (MMR), Philippines 2017 (PHL), Thailand 2015–16 (THA), Vietnam 2014 (VNM)

Source: Calculated using data from Demographic Health Surveys (DHS) and Multiple Indicator Cluster Surveys (MICS).

migrants—women from Vietnam, the Philippines, and Indonesia migrate to destination countries both within and outside the region, including Hong Kong, Korea, Singapore, and Taiwan. Marriage remains the dominant form of union, with low levels of cohabitation except in the Philippines. In the Philippines, cohabitation rates have quadrupled over the last two decades, with nearly a quarter of all young women in a cohabiting union primarily due to socio-economic disadvantages (Kuang et al. 2019).

Divorce is becoming more common. Without exception, throughout the region, divorce rates have increased (Dommaraju and Jones 2011). In Vietnam, divorce rates doubled in just a decade between 2000 and 2010, mainly driven by higher divorce rates among young couples (Tran 2016). The pattern in Vietnam is typical of the changes happening in the rest of the region. Even in Islamic Southeast Asia, where divorce rates began to decline in the 1960s, the trend has reversed and divorce rates started to increase in the 1990s (Jones 2017). With rising divorce rates, the pool of people available to remarry has expanded. As remarriages were common in much of the region, there has likely been an increase in the number of remarriages as well. However, demographic data on remarriages are lacking for countries in the region.

DEMOGRAPHIC CHANGES AND THE FAMILY STRUCTURE

The demographic changes described above influence families in multiple ways. Changing marriage patterns have delayed family formation. Young people are likely to spend more time in their parents' homes. With delayed marriage and increasing non-marriage, family structure is changing to include fictive kins. Divorce and remarriage create complex family transitions with new kinship ties and family structures, including blended or single-parent families (Balachandran and Yeung 2020). Divorces could also lead to the formation of intergenerational families as divorced mothers with children move back to their parental homes, as seen in Vietnam (Tran 2016). Transnational marriages are likely to transform family values, identities, and subjectivities.

Declining births have a direct impact on household size. As seen in Figure 2.2, in all countries in the region with available data, the average household size has declined. Household size is determined by

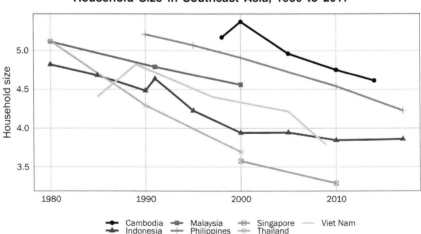

FIGURE 2.2
Household Size in Southeast Asia, 1980 to 2017

Source: Based on data from United Nations (2019c)

births and other demographic trends, including union formation and dissolution (Jiang and O'Neill 2007). The contribution of the different demographic components to the decline in household size in the region has yet to be examined. Such declines have implications on family functions, household savings and consumption, and the welfare of household members, including care arrangements.

Migration, both internal and international, creates new family structures. Changes in economic and labour opportunities have led to "delocalisation of living" and "disembedding of households", especially in rural areas (Rigg et al. 2012). Migration could potentially lead to family division, but it could also lead to co-residence. Whether migration leads to multigenerational households in the region is typically influenced, among other factors, by housing cost and affordability (Esteve and Liu 2018). Global householding and transnational families are a natural outgrowth of international migration in the region. Such households and families take different forms, but all face unique challenges, from marital stability to issues related to citizenship, child welfare, and support of left-behind family members.

Increasing life expectancy brings to the forefront living arrangements and family structures of older people. Intergenerational living arrangements in the region are much more common than in East Asia. However, living arrangements are only one aspect of the family. As United Nations (2017) has noted, living arrangements do not adequately capture the flows and direction of support across generations which is often determined by the needs and capacities of different generations. As life expectancy has increased, the time spent in grandparenthood has increased. In the context of migration and the need for intensive childrearing practices, older people play a vital role in grandparenting in the region (Dommaraju and Wong 2022)

The current household structure in the region is presented in Figure 2.3. The predominant type of families in the region are couples living with children, reaching close to 50 per cent in Vietnam. This form of nuclear household was common in the past, suggesting a remarkable stability and resilience of nuclear households in the face of demographic transitions (Dommaraju and Tan 2014). In other regions of Asia, nucleation of families is seen as a shift from the intergenerational structures of the past. However, in Southeast Asia, where nuclear households have historically been prevalent, the focus should be on their persistence rather than shift or convergence.

The next typical type of family structure is the extended family, which makes up more than 30 per cent of households. Extended

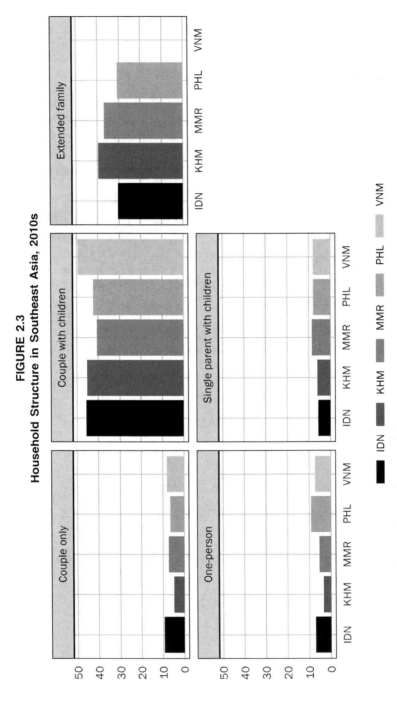

households could include stem families with parents/parents-in-law, son/daughter-in-law, or grandchildren. They could also include other family members such as uncles, aunts, nieces, and nephews. Figure 2.4 presents the prevalence of intergenerational living in the region. Between 15 and 25 per cent of households are composed of members of three generations, with the lowest rate in Vietnam and the highest in Cambodia. The bilateral kinship system in the region allows flexibility in post-marital living arrangements, which makes intergenerational living much more common.

Skipped generational households refer to households in which the middle generation is missing. This could include households with grandparents and grandchildren but without children. These types of households in the region often result from migration of parents, although they could also arise due to parental death (Ingersoll-Dayton et al. 2020). Such households are more common in rural areas compared to urban areas. Grandparents are seen as playing a crucial role by taking care of grandchildren, thus allowing parents to migrate. Studies on skipped generational households in the region have focused on the well-being of children and grandparents in such households formed due to migration (Teerawichitchainan 2021).

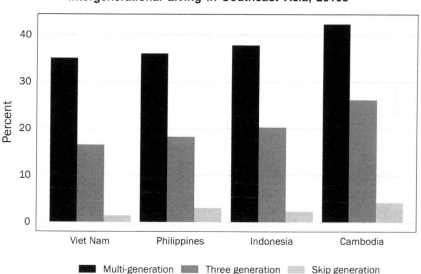

FIGURE 2.4
Intergenerational Living in Southeast Asia, 2010s

Source: Based on data from United Nations (2019c)

Single-parent families, predominantly mothers with children, are close to or above 8 per cent of households in Myanmar, Vietnam, and the Philippines. Marital dissolution or migration often result in single-parent families. Whether migration or marital dissolution will lead to single-parent families depends on the prevailing norms and contexts of the different countries. These events could result in the formation of multigenerational households if the parents decide to move to their natal homes. As divorce becomes more common, there is likely opportunity for an increase in this form of household. In contrast to other parts of the world, however, single-parent households due to out of wedlock birth remain low.

Between 5 and 10 per cent of households in the region are couple-only households. These households fall into two categories. Younger married couples who have not started their childbearing and older people whose children no longer stay with them.

The last category of household is a one-person household. The proportion of one-person households varies between 3 and 10 per cent. In Thailand, for which no recent data are available, the percentage is likely to be even higher. Those living alone follow age and gendered patterns. The first group of those living alone are younger adults who are not staying with their family for work or study-related reasons. The other group are older people living alone. Older women predominate in this category as they are likely to outlive their spouse.

The patterns described here offer a static view of families in the region. As observed by Dommaraju and Tan (2014), families in the region are far from static. Family composition changes throughout the life course of an individual with addition or exit of family members from the household. Changes to families are not only influenced by cultural values and norms that vary across the societies in the region, but also reflect changing desires, economic and other constraints faced by individuals and families.

FAMILY CHANGES FROM AN INDIVIDUAL PERSPECTIVE

Changes in the family can be examined from the perspective of individuals. Figure 2.5 takes an individual perspective to illustrate the changes in family structure in the Philippines between 1990 and 2010. The first panel shows the percentage of people living in a household with no other family members by age group. Such single-person households are prevalent at younger and older ages. At other ages, the prevalence is very low at about 2 per cent. There has been

FIGURE 2.5
Family Structure in the Philippines: Individual Perspective, 1990 and 2010

A. Living without any family member

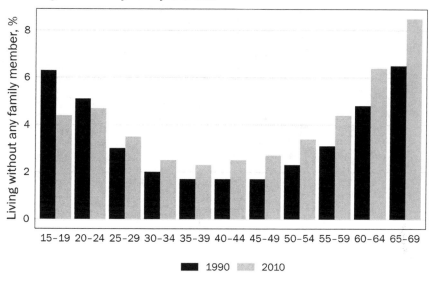

B. Living with mother

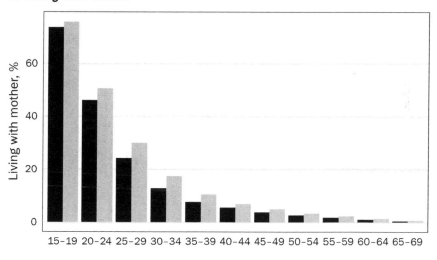

C. Living with spouse

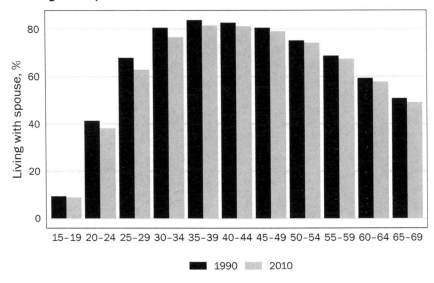

D. Living with children

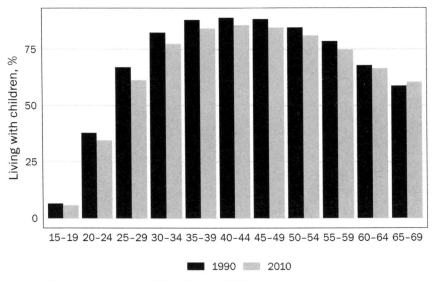

Source: Based on data from United Nations (2019c).

an increase in single-person households, especially for those at older ages; but for those aged 15–19 there has been a decline over time. This suggest that younger adults have delayed leaving their parental home until at least their early 20s.

The next panel shows the percentage living in a household with their mother present. For those aged 15–19, this reaches nearly 70 per cent, rapidly declining beyond the 20s as individuals marry and form their own households. Interestingly, over time, the percentage of children living with their mothers has increased at younger ages suggesting later leaving of parental homes or forming of extended households. In the next panel, we see the percentage living with a spouse. This type of living peaks in the early 40s. Changes suggest a slight decline at younger ages but nearly identical patterns at middle age and beyond. The final panel is on living with children: nearly three-fourths of individuals aged between 30 and 60 were living with their children. Over time, like living with a spouse, though there has been a decline at younger ages, at middle age and beyond the trend in living with children does not appear to have changed much.

The illustration in the case of the Philippines points to changes that might also be happening elsewhere in the region. These changes include a growing proportion of older people living without any family member, delays in leaving home among the young, decline in those living with a spouse or children at younger ages. However, the region is heterogenous in marriage, fertility, migration, and mortality patterns, and individual patterns shown for the Philippines might not apply. In countries such as Thailand, which have seen a much more rapid demographic transition, the effect on the family could be much more pronounced.

CONCLUSION

The chapter highlighted some of the current patterns in families and households and their links to demographic changes in the region. The transformation of family structures is not unique to the region. Across the world, households are being transformed by migration, labour opportunities, social and normative changes (Spiker et al. 2011). These transformations affect individuals of all ages—from children to older people. As families continue to be a key institution in the region, any changes to the family structure could impact well-being of individuals.

The countries in the region are at different stages of demographic transition. Therefore, some countries have a younger population while others are moving towards a rapidly ageing population. For countries with a younger population, family structures have to adjust to later marriage and later leaving of homes by young adults. For countries with an increasingly older population, the extended family support system that older people could depend on in the past is fraying. The demographic, normative, and economic changes are leading to renegotiation and reinterpreting of intergenerational obligations. Older people face the challenge of disempowerment and discrimination in the labour market that favours younger workers, with the labour market itself segmented by age. Older people in the region face precarious incomes in an increasingly unequal economic system.

For older women in the region, the vulnerabilities are further heightened. Though the region is known to be much more gender egalitarian compared to its South or East Asian neighbours, ageing experience is deeply gendered. In demographic parlance, ageing is feminized as there are more older women than men due to persistent gender inequalities in life expectancy. Women in the region enter old age with disadvantages cumulated over their life course. The disadvantages faced by older women are intrinsically entwined with the experiences they had throughout their life course. Women's rights concerning property, maintenance, and support are often challenging to enforce. Women disproportionately are engaged in care work—at younger ages caring for children and at older ages caring for their spouse, grandchildren, or other family members (Devashayam 2014). As such work is not financially compensated, women at older ages are at increased risk of dependency on family for support. Widowed and divorced women face an even higher risk of income insecurity at older ages.

Demographic shifts and associated changes to the family have deepened the need for supporting policies and welfare measures from the state. However, state policies in the region have often relied on the family as the first and prime institution to provide support and welfare to its members. Rather than assisting the family, states in the region have primarily sought to minimize their role in dealing with demographic and family transitions. There are hardly any policies to tackle, for instance, the welfare needs of transnational marriage migrants who face systemic inequalities in the legal system and citizenship rights. Institutional provisions to deal with challenges faced by divorced families, single-person households, or children growing up in skipped generational households are also lacking. For older people many countries in the region have launched action plans but they have not been backed up by serious financial commitment or reforms to existing structures and policies including those dealing with income security at older ages.

REFERENCES

Badan Pusat Statistik. 2015. *Population of Indonesia: Results of the 2015 Intercensal Population Survey*. Statistics Indonesia.

Balachandran, Lavanya and Wei-Jun Jean Yeung. 2020. "Old Bonds, New Ties: Contextualizing Family Transitions in Re-partnerships, Remarriage and Stepfamilies in Asia". *Journal of Family Issues* 41, no. 7: 879–90. https://doi.org/10.1177/0192513x20918428.

Basten, Stuart, Sergei Scherbov, and Warren Sanderson. 2015. "Remeasuring Ageing in Southeast Asia". *Asian Population Studies* 11, no. 2: 191–210. https://doi.org/10.1080/17441730.2015.1052201.

Devasahayam, Theresa W. 2014. "Gender and Ageing. What do We Know about Gender?" In *Gender and Ageing: Southeast Asian Perspectives*, edited by Theresa W. Devashayam, pp. 1–31. Singapore: Institute of Southeast Asian Studies.

Dommaraju, Premchand and Gavin Jones. 2011. "Divorce Trends in Asia". *Asian Journal of Social Science* 39, no. 6: 725–50. https://doi.org/10.1163/156853111x619201.

Dommaraju, Premchand and JooEan Tan. 2014. "Households in Contemporary Southeast Asia". *Journal of Comparative Family Studies* 45, no. 4: 559–80. https://doi.org/10.3138/jcfs.45.4.559.

Dommaraju, Premchand and Shawn Wong. 2022. "Grandparenthood and Grandparenting in Asia". In *Handbook of Aging, Health and Public Policy*, edited by I. Rajan. Singapore: Springer Nature. https://doi.org/10.1007/978-981-16-1914-4_40-1.

Esteve, Albert and Chia Liu. 2018. "Families in Asia: A Cross-national Comparison of Household-size and Co-residence". In *Routledge Handbook of Asian Demography*, edited by Zhongwei Zhao and Adrian C. Hayes, pp. 370–93. Routledge.

Farris, D. Nicole. 2020. "Introduction: The Demography of Marriage and Family". In *International Handbook on the Demography of Marriage and the Family*, edited by D. Nicole Farris and A. Bourque. Springer. https://doi.org/10.1007/978-3-030-35079-6_1.

Fong, Eric and Kumiko Shibuya. 2020. "Migration Patterns in East and Southeast Asia: Causes and Consequences". *Annual Review of Sociology* 46, no. 1: 1–21. https://doi.org/10.1146/annurev-soc-121919-054644.

Hull, Terence H. 2012. "Fertility in Southeast Asia". In *Demographic Change in Southeast Asia: Recent Histories and Future Directions*, edited by Lindy Williams and Michael Philip Guest, pp. 43–64. Cornell Southeast Asia Programme. Ithaca, New York: Cornell University.

Ingersoll-Dayton, Berit, Kanchana Tangchonlatip, and Sureeporn Punpuing. 2020. "A Confluence of Worries: Grandparents in Skipped-generation Households in Thailand". *Journal of Family Issues* 41, no. 2: 135–57. https://doi.org/10.1177/0192513X19868836.

IOM. 2021. Global Migration Data Portal. https://migrationdataportal.org/regional-data-overview/south-eastern-asia.

Jiang, Leiwen and Brian C. O'Neill. 2007. "Impacts of Demographic Trends on US Household Size and Structure". *Population and Development Review* 33: 567–91. https://doi.org/10.1111/j.1728-4457.2007.00186.x.

Jones, Gavin W. 2017. "Changing Marriage Patterns in Asia". In *Routledge Handbook of Asian Demography*, edited by Zhongwei Zhao and Adrian C. Hayes, pp. 351–69. Routledge.

Jones, Gavin W. and Premchand Dommaraju. 2012. "Rural Demography in Asia and the Pacific Rim". In *International Handbook of Rural Demography*, edited by László J. Kulcsár and Katherine J. Curtis, pp. 111–24. Springer. https://doi.org/10.1007/978-94-007-1842-5_9.

Jones, Gavin W. and Wei-Jun Jean Yeung. 2014. "Marriage in Asia". *Journal of Family Issues*, 35, no. 12: 1567–83. https://doi.org/10.1177/0192513x14538029.

Kuang, Bernice, Brienna Perelli-Harris, and Sabu Padmadas. 2019. "The Unexpected Rise of Cohabitation in the Philippines: Evidence of Socioeconomic Disadvantage or a Second Demographic Transition?" *Asian Population Studies* 15, no. 1: 8–27. https://doi.org/10.1080/17441730.2018.1560664.

Rigg, Jonathan, Albert Salamanca, and Michael Parnwell. 2012. "Joining the Dots of Agrarian Change in Asia: A 25 Year View from Thailand". *World Development* 40, no. 7: 1469–81.

Teerawichitchainan, Bussarawan and Timothy Qing Ying Low. 2021. "The Situation and Well-being of Custodial Grandparents in Myanmar: Impacts of Adult Children's Cross-border and Internal Migration". *Social Science & Medicine* 277. https://doi.org/10.1016/j.socscimed.2021.113914.

Tey, Nai Peng. 2017. "Southeast Asia's Demographic Situation, Regional Variations, and National Challenges". In *Southeast Asian Affairs 2017*, edited by Daljit Singh and Malcolm Cook, pp. 55–82. Singapore: ISEAS – Yusof Ishak Institute. https://doi.org/10.1355/9789814762878-007.

Tran, Thi Ming Thi. 2016. "Prevalence and Patterns of Divorce in Vietnam: Tradition, Modernity, and Individualism". *Journal of Literature and Art Studies* 6, no. 3: 298–316. https://doi.org/10.17265/2159-5836/2016.03.010.

UNESCAP. 2017. *Addressing the Challenges of Population Ageing in Asia and the Pacific: Implementation of the Madrid International Plan of Action on Ageing.* Bangkok: United Nations.

United Nations. 2017. *Living Arrangements of Older Persons: A Report on an Expanded International Dataset.* New York: Department of Economic and Social Affairs, Population Division, United Nations.

———. 2018. *World Urbanization Prospects: The 2018 Revision.* New York: Department of Economic and Social Affairs, Population Division, United Nations.

———. 2019a. *World Marriage Data 2019.* New York: Department of Economic and Social Affairs, Population Division, United Nations.

———. 2019b. *World Population Prospects 2019.* New York: Department of Economic and Social Affairs, Population Division, United Nations.

———. 2019c. *Database on Household Size and Composition 2019.* New York: Department of Economic and Social Affairs, Population Division, United Nations.

Yeung, Wei-Jun Jean and Hu Su. 2018. *Family and Population Changes in Singapore: A Unique Case in Global Family Change.* London: Routledge.

Yeung, Wei-Jun Jean and Zheng Mu. 2019. "Migration and Marriage in Asian Contexts". *Journal of Ethnic and Migration Studies* 46, no. 14: 1–17. https://doi.org/10.1080/1369183x.2019.1585005.

3

NEW NORMAL, OLD TIES: COVID-19'S SOCIAL IMPACT ON THE SINGAPORE-JOHOR BAHRU CONNECTION

Kevin S.Y. Tan and Grace Lim

OLD NEIGHBOURS

Singaporeans and Malaysians share a common social-cultural and political past. In fact, the origins of their respective sovereignties are highly entwined with each other (Baker 2014; Shiraishi 2008). This is because from 1963, the two countries were part of the same nation for almost two years. However, due to increasing political differences and ethnic tensions, Singapore was accorded an independence from 1965 that was never entirely planned nor self-determined. Nevertheless, in spite of political separation, the ties that have bounded their citizens have continued in the areas of economy, culture and even sports (Little 2013, pp. 635–51). A tangible testimony to such ties is best revealed when one observes the porous nature of the borderlands connection (Chan and Womack 2016, pp. 95–103) between the two countries, where continuing flows of labour, income and resources have contributed to the subsequent growth and development of Singapore and Johor Bahru (Hampton 2010, pp. 239–53; Hutchinson and Rahman 2020), the closest Malaysian city to Singapore. Rather than existing simply as a boundary, the border checkpoints and the lands adjacent to them express varying levels of liminality (Kurki 2014, p. 1061). An essential component that has enabled this is the existence of two causeways, or bridges, which connect Singapore's much smaller island-state to the rest of the peninsula occupied by its larger neighbour, Malaysia.

These two causeways connect Singapore to the southern tip of Peninsula Malaysia via Johor Bahru across the Straits of Johor. They enable travel over a body of water that stretches from 1.5 kilometres to 4.8 kilometres at this widest point. While both causeways serve similar functions, they vary in terms of their relative age. The far older Woodlands Causeway first became accessible for cross-straits traffic on 1 October 1923, but was only officially opened the following year on 11 June 1924 after full completion (Chua 2009). Even till present times, it has been referred to as "The Causeway" or the "Woodlands Causeway" by locals on both sides of the border. The second and comparatively newer bridge, is better known as the "Tuas Second Link" and it officially began operating on 18 April 1998 as part of efforts to lessen the burgeoning human traffic at the older Woodlands Causeway (Lim Tin Seng 2020). In spite of this second causeway, however, the traffic on either of them, especially on weekends and public holidays, has been notorious for its sheer volume. Prior to the COVID-19 pandemic, on average between 300,000 to 400,000 persons (Chong et al. 2017) were commuting between Johor Bahru to Singapore on weekdays for employment. The bulk of the traffic on weekdays often consisted of Malaysians who enter Singapore for employment on work permits. On weekends or public holidays, however, more Singaporeans cross over, often regarding Johor Bahru as a convenient and affordable site for short-term tourism.

When it comes to the mode of transport for going across either the Woodlands Causeway or the Second Link, there are a number of options. One can drive a personal vehicle; take a train; take public transport on buses; or even choose to walk across. Based on observations, some have also used their own personal urban mobility devices such as skate-scooters or motorized bicycles in place of walking. The option to walk can be perilous if undertaken under a hot sun and heavy traffic, but on the other hand, can be a very pleasant walk from the Malaysian side just before dawn under a cool and clear sky, as thousands rush to work on a weekday morning. During weekday rush hours, commuters taking buses on weekends can take up to two hours before they cross the border. The train, on the other hand, operated by Malaysia's KTM (Keretapi Tanah Melayu), is often in high demand resulting in tickets often sold out, due to its relatively hassle free and short journey of under five minutes either direction. Finally, driving a personal vehicle across is relatively the most comfortable approach as one can avoid facing large crowds, although the use of motorcycles on the other hand can be a gruelling experience in view of the heavy traffic (Ong and Amir 2018; Ye 2016).

Regardless of one's mode of transport, commuting over the two causeways during peak hours often results in transport bottlenecks and long delays that is especially time consuming. These negotiated physical mobilities (Larsen et al. 2006; Urry 2007) contextualize what Hodgson (2011, pp. 41–64) refers to as "structures of encounterability" where travel, identity and networks are part of a broader process of community development. Such structures are further exacerbated by how both customs checkpoints on either side, particularly on the Malaysian side, have become increasingly under strain in terms of their capacity to hand the heavy traffic, especially on weekends. With the volume of persons traversing these two causeways expected to increase in the future, there have been suggestions in recent years to construct a third link (*Channel NewsAsia* 2018). More recently, plans for a Rapid Transit System (RTS), linking the Woodlands North MRT station in Singapore to Bukit Chagar just next to the Sultan Iskandar CIQ Complex in Johor is underway, and has been targeted to be operational from 2027. However, what happened during 2020 to 2022 at the height of the COVID-19 pandemic, is a sober reminder that such plans may not always be guaranteed.

AN UNPRECEDENTED CLOSURE

Due to the COVID-19 coronavirus pandemic, transborder travel between the countries via the two causeways was seriously affected. At the stroke of midnight on 18 March 2020 (Yong et al. 2020), the land borders between Singapore and Malaysia were shut down. This was an unprecedented event since the Second World War, ending a decades-long land passageway between Singapore and Malaysia. Although the virus had first emerged in Thailand at the start of 2020, it had become apparent by mid-March that the COVID-19 coronavirus was oblivious to political boundaries. Numerous clusters of infected persons had already emerged in various locations in Peninsula Malaysia in a matter of days, with several appearing to be linked to a major religious event known as a *Tablighi Jamaat*, which was held from 27 February to 1 March 2020 in Kuala Lumpur (Hadi and Zam 2020). In spite of initial hopes that the infections would not grow, the number of persons already infected with COVID-19 were past 500 by 16 March 2020. This became the breaking point for the Malaysian Government, leading them to put in place a nationwide Movement Control Order (MCO) to curb the rapid surge in infections. It would be the first of a series of varying MCOs to be put in place over the next nineteen months till October 2021 (Chu 2021).

At the time when the first MCO was implemented in Malaysia, the situation in Singapore was not as serious but concern and uncertainty was growing. By mid-March 2020, there were close to 250 cases on the island-state—half of the Malaysian cases—but the Malaysian surge foreshadowed what was to come for Singapore. By the start of April 2020, cases of COVID-19 infection exceeded 1,000 in Singapore, leading to the implementation of Singapore's own national lockdown on 7 April, which was also named "Circuit Breaker". This lasted for over two months till mid-June 2020, when the Singapore government announced a new phased approach to restoring a sense of normalcy similar to pre-pandemic times. It would be for almost two years until 1 April 2022 when the borders will be fully reopened again for both countries.

LIFE UNDER LOCKDOWN

During the initial months of the lockdowns on either side, many Singaporeans and Malaysians were inevitably trapped on both sides of the causeways. An estimated number of around 100,000 Malaysians remained in Singapore during this period as many had to eventually choose between prolonged separation from their families or to remain at their better salaried Singapore-based jobs (Chia 2021). Many chose the latter at the cost of a prolonged liminal state that created precarious income security. On social media platforms such as Facebook, a public discussion group known as "Malaysia-Singapore Border Crossers"[1] grew to a membership size of more than 136,000 members in a matter of weeks since the initial closure of the causeways, providing both information and mutual support for persons not being able to return to either country. The discussion group's content was replete with videos, pictures and comments articulating the challenges of living apart from family and loved ones.

The nationwide MCO that the Malaysian government had initially imposed allowed only cargo and food supplies through the borders. As approximately hundreds of thousands of Malaysians cross either one of the causeways as part of their daily commute to school or employment, it goes without being said, just how significant an impact that the closure would have on the lives of so many. This is because, according to records, the growth of migrant labour from Malaysia to Singapore had risen by five times from 1990 to 2019, a trend largely driven by the preference of the stronger Singapore dollar and the potentially better quality of life that might arise due to it (*Today* 2016). Many often took up jobs that were shunned by Singaporeans. This was acceptable to many Malaysians, as they could find incomes in Singapore that paid them nearly three times their salary back home (*Straits Times* 2017), although it was made possible at great costs to personal well-being due to the challenges of the daily commute (Lim 2018).

For the Malaysians remaining in Singapore, affordable accommodation became a challenge. Facing the immediate border closure since March 2020, the Singapore government had taken action to facilitate the supply of temporary housing alongside private companies. Grants were provided to reduce the cost of accommodation on employers and Malaysian Work Pass Holders, offering up to $50 per employee, capped at 14 days (Wong 2020). Some Singaporean businesses also stepped in to provide free short term accommodation support. Despite the extensive support offered during this period, many Malaysians continued to face the high costs of accommodation while in Singapore. Businesses on both sides took a severe hit during the pandemic, and many had to resort to placing employees on unpaid leave or firing them. One of the first casualties would be nightspots and the entertainment industry on either side of the border.

While subsidies had been provided by the Malaysian government to support businesses during the pandemic, many of its citizens were left out of the protection circle. Retrenched Malaysians or those under indefinite unpaid leave while remaining in Singapore were unable to seek part-time jobs due to the local labour law. At the same time, many could not return to Malaysia due to Singapore's circuit breaker lockdown. Consequently, many Malaysian workers on the island-state were left to their own devices, bearing the costs of securing and renting accommodation in the midst of the pandemic. During this period, Rahman (2021) noted that Johor's poverty rate rose from 3.9 per cent in 2019 to almost 8 per cent in 2020, together with a sharp rise in suicides. While many favoured staying in Singapore to wait for a new job, they remained highly vulnerable to changes in pandemic-related government policies. In the initial weeks after the closure of the borders, among those who chose to remain in Singapore, there were reports (Nabilah 2020) of Malaysian workers stranded in Singapore and sleeping in the open areas of MRT[2] stations.

Growing economic precarity among citizens was a growing concern on both sides. Singaporean businesses that had always been reliant on Malaysian labour commuting across the border daily faced a shortage in labour supply as they struggled to coordinate the manpower shortages given limited timeframes. In particular, renovation firms were one of the hardest hit industries, as Malaysians working in the industry made up approximately 80 per cent of its skilled workforce (Tan undated). The border lockdowns, however, have resulted in more than a 10 per cent decline in the number of foreign nationals in Singapore, of which Malaysians constitute a large part of (Loh 2021). The majority of Malaysians commuting via the causeway daily have been employed under work permits[3] and they experienced the sharpest decline in employment rate following the onset of the lockdowns.

During the border closures at the height of the pandemic from 2020–21, numerous reports highlighted the emotional and mental toll that the lockdowns placed on families that were separated. This was because travelling to either side due to familial reasons was regarded as "non-essential travel", and only reasons pertaining to business or diplomacy were considered otherwise. Entire families were kept apart—parents separated from their children; spouses involuntarily kept away from each other for months; and on a few tragic occasions, family members passed away without an opportunity to see their loved ones a final time. This reflected how the initial decision to either return to one's own country or to remain at "the other side" was often a difficult one and multifactorial, while the costs in making them were not only economically but also psychologically challenging.

For those with translocalized lives on both sides of the border, the so-called "new normal" presented significant challenges in terms of caregiving. Persons had to put their education on hold in order to care for their loved ones (Amir 2021a). Another report during the initial months of the initial lockdown revealed how up to 350 Malaysian mothers with new-born babies in Johor Bahru but were stuck in Singapore collectively engaged a Malaysian-based forwarding company to deliver breast milk across the border to their children (Tho 2020). Later that same year in October 2020, up to 20 Malaysian families consisting of up to 50 persons engaged a yacht with the help of a local developer for rides along the Straits of Johor to view and wave to their loved ones on the Singaporean shoreline near the Woodlands Causeway (Ong 2020). This event showed just how powerful socially constructed boundaries between spaces can be in the context of international borders. The continued separation of persons in such cases can be frustrating, especially when one's family members are mere metres away but remain unreachable. It was also a reflection of just how much the land passage via the causeways between Singapore and Johor Bahru has become such an indelible part of everyday life for Singaporeans and Malaysians.

THE TRANSLOCAL QUALITY OF SINGAPORE AND JOHOR BAHRU TIES

The two causeways, therefore, represent a deep and ongoing connection that goes well beyond the distinct political boundaries between Malaysia and Singapore as nation-states. From an economic and social-cultural point of view, this is certainly most pronounced in the specific case of Johor Bahru's high reliance on the role of Singaporean tourists and their real estate investments that have contributed to the overall position of Johor being Malaysia's 4th richest state in terms of Gross Domestic Product[4]. The urbanization of Johor Bahru has also been reliant on a corresponding growth occurring in Singapore, having evolved into a sort of "dual city" of the latter (Nasongkhla and Sintusingha 2013, pp. 1836–53). Economic growth on both sides and the sustainability of many essential services (especially in Singapore) has always been made possible by this continued relationship.

For many Malaysians in Johor Bahru, having easy access to Singapore has also been an important opportunity for an overall better quality of life, particularly among those of Chinese and Indian ethnicity who may be dissatisfied with the racially differentiated form of citizenship in their own country (Koh 2015, pp. 531–50). As a result, the experience of everyday life involves an undeniable *translocal* quality for many Malaysians who commute back and forth the causeways almost daily, a common phenomenon observed in similar borderlands studies among scholars (Wilson 2012). This is where territoriality and intersectionality stand in tension with each other as the assigned international boundaries that divide borderlands between distinct countries are often more porous and interdependent than assumed in political narrative. At the same time, one should not assume that such porosity implies a homogenous and egalitarian relationship between borderlands. These complex relations between the spaces surrounding a border can be highly nuanced and uneven. Such interdependency is correspondingly reflected among Singaporeans who view Johor Bahru as an alternative and advantageous space for home ownership, education, recreation, healthcare and even retirement, such as in sites like Iskandar, the southern development corridor of Johor (Razak et al. 2016, pp. 121–34; Rizzo and Khan 2013, pp. 154–62), where it was also once heralded as a key part of the "Growth Triangle" in ASEAN (Awang et al. 1998).

To place all this in perspective, the typical cost of a brand new three-bedroom apartment within Singapore's public housing system, in recent years, can exceed $450,000 Singapore dollars in certain prime locations. In practice, this is considered a lease rather than true ownership of the apartment as the government has the right to reclaim it within 99 years. In Johor Bahru, however, Singaporeans are able to purchase their own larger and freehold condominium unit with amenities, starting from a minimum of one million Malaysian Ringgit[5], which is approximately $300,000 Singapore dollars at the time of writing. Such advantages are further supported by the My Malaysia Second Home (MMSH) programme[6] that was specifically put in place to further foreign investment into the Malaysian property market. In recent years, reports of disabled or elderly Singaporeans who require nursing support, but have been unable to cope with the costs in their home country, have also sought out Johor Bahru as a practical option (Tai et al. 2015). In addition, the emergence of EduCity in Johor's

Iskandar Puteri has also been offering degree programmes run by established western universities at a fraction of what they could cost in Singapore (Yang 2016).

Correspondingly, prior to the start of the COVID-19 pandemic, up to half a million or more Malaysians either live or commute regularly to Singapore for employment on weekdays, while returning via the causeways to their homes in Johor Bahru or further locations in the Malaysian Peninsula. Prior to the emergence of the COVID-19 pandemic at the end of 2019, it was estimated that there were at least 952,261 Malaysians or Singaporean citizens with Malaysian origins residing in Singapore (United Nations 2019). And as mentioned earlier, during weekends or public holidays, thousands of Singaporeans also take the opportunity for day trips or short getaways to Johor Bahru to maximize their superior currency through the purchase of goods and services.

Johor Bahru, therefore, has become a cheaper alternative for dealing with the increasing cost of living for many Singaporeans, particularly those coming from more modest socio-economic backgrounds. Such "weekenders" cross the causeways for visits that last only just four to five hours or overnight stays before returning. The reasons for the journey range from getting a budget car wash, filling up the petrol tank of one's car, the purchase of affordable groceries and sundries, and even to enjoy the culinary treats at the endless number of restaurants and street food vendors that are not as easily found in Singapore. In addition, relatively more affordable sites for recreation and entertainment such as cinemas, theme parks (i.e. Hello Kitty Town[7]) and even golf courses beckon. This also includes access to affordable therapeutic massages, KTV bars and personal services for some Singaporeans with certain sensual needs.[8]

In view of such realities, it would be simplistic to assume that the reasons for such "reverse-mobilities" of Singaporeans into Johor Bahru are purely economic. Some Singaporeans view occasional travel to Johor Bahru as a much needed existential break from the hustle and bustle of their island-nation, where long work hours prevail amidst the stress of an achievement-oriented ethos that is tightly bureaucratic and rationalized in the Weberian sense. This has led to the emergence of a large modern shopping mall virtually next to the Malaysian Customs Checkpoint at the Woodlands Causeway known as "City Square Mall" since 1999 (Zazali 2005). Prior to the COVID-19 pandemic, the mall had been a bustling destination for many Singaporeans on weekends looking for a quick "shop and return" retail adventure within a day. The comments from a Singaporean we encountered reflect similar sentiments:

> ... the pace of life in Johor is more relaxed. We are not constantly rushing for things. I know friends who have properties here, and use it for their weekend home ... we can get away from the rat race of Singapore. Because the housing estates ... more space ... creating an atmosphere with room to breathe ... Some with children will use a home to chill out after travelling to Johor's tourist destinations. There's a lot more to see and do in Johor than Singapore.
>
> — *Esther is in her thirties and works in an educational institution in Singapore, but had been living in Masai, Johor Bahru for more than ten years.*

Discussions in recent years among both formal and informal sources often lead to conclusions about how Johor Bahru is far more "relaxed" or "easy-going" as compared to life in Singapore. Due to its relatively slower rate of urbanization, the draw for Johor Bahru for many Singaporeans is the opportunity to relive a certain "older-world" charm that they have lamented to be increasingly difficult to reclaim in their own country. Home ownership in Johor Bahru has, in many ways, become an alternate means of the realizing hopes and dreams for a quality of life among Singaporeans who, during their lifetimes, would not have been able to achieve in their own country. This is in view of the rapid rising costs of living on the island-state and perceived growing socio-economic inequalities within its society. By mid-2022, the exchange value of the Singapore dollar was worth more than three Malaysian Ringgit, and has continued to hover at such a rate. This has obviously made Johor Bahru a prime location for investment in real estate, even for Singaporeans with more modest means.

At the same time, while it has been argued that Malaysia's relatively lower wages were an attempt by its government to increase the country's competitive positioning to the global economy, such progress has been closely related to Singapore's economic restructuring in the 1970s, marking the start of the island-state's strategic reliance on foreign labour. Although there have been attempts to increase the pool of skilled foreign labour as part of the government's strategy of driving the economic competitiveness of Singapore, Malaysian migrant labour typically remains concentrated among work permit holders, often in the manufacturing, construction, janitorial, security, retail and food industries (Lay 2022). To a significant extent, many exist precariously as part of broader regional migrant labour flows that might prove uncertain and dangerous due to their disempowered status (Bastide 2015, pp. 226–45).

In 2014, Malaysians reportedly took up 370,000 work permit licenses, out of 770,000, making them an invaluable part of Singapore's workforce (TCW2 2014). As Malaysians have consistently been the largest migrant population in Singapore (United Nations Department of Economic and Social Affairs undated; Yang et. al 2017, pp. 10–25), the border closure from 2020–22 has led to sustained obstacles to the livelihood of several hundreds of thousands of them, particularly those who have depended on employment in Singapore in either low-wage manual work or even as better-paid skilled professionals in a broad range of industries. Consequently, this has been a reason to encourage Malaysians to either seek Permanent Residency or Citizenship status in Singapore in order to have access to even better paid jobs. For many, the decision to eventually become a Singaporean citizen is attractive in view of perceived racial inequalities in Malaysia. This may be seen as part of the reason why Malaysians accounted for up to 44 per cent of foreign-born Singapore citizens just prior to the COVID-19 pandemic (Lim 2020).

ATTEMPTS TO REOPEN THE BORDER

By the third quarter of 2020, it was increasingly apparent that the extended lockdown would be untenable in the long run. By near the end of the Singaporean "Circuit Breaker" period in 2020, hundreds of thousands of Malaysians employed across the non-essential sector were in limbo over their job status as many retail and services outlets ceased operations (Yang 2020). The positive news at the time, however, was that infections on either side had apparently subsided, leaving some room for a gradual relaxing of restrictions. During September 2020, therefore, almost six months into the closure of the land border due to the COVID-19 pandemic, efforts were made to create a Periodic Commuting Arrangement (PCA) and a Reciprocal Green Lane (RGL) to enable persons to traverse the border for employment or business-related activities.

The PCA and the RGL were the first attempts to enable cross-border travel, although they were highly limited. The PCA, with its implementation of a quarantine period of seven days was an attempt to facilitate travel for Malaysians to return to work in Singapore while the RGL was put in place in an agreement with selected countries that were deemed to have controlled their infections. The latter enabled short-term travel of up to 14 days for essential and official business while the former allowed for the entry of residents of both countries who hold valid work passes. All this was put in place on 17 August 2020, but the measures were revised again in November 2020 owing to another spike in COVID-19 cases, leading to the eventual suspension of these schemes on 1 February 2021. The following months till the final quarter of 2021 saw the onset of second and third waves of COVID-19 infections that greatly reduced traffic along the causeways to just the flow of essential goods and services.

Nevertheless on 3 May 2021, borders were reportedly set to reopen to facilitate travels for compassionate reasons under the Compassionate Travel Scheme. This comes after reports of strained family ties following the prolonged 13-month border closure along with growing appeals by citizens on both sides. The RCL and PCA schemes were also set to resume. Although Malaysian workers in Singapore were by then able to travel across the border, the situation did not improve much for them. This is because while the PCA provides the option for workers to take a short trip back to Malaysia to be with their families, many Singaporean employers were unwilling to fork out the estimated $2,000 fee for their quarantine. Staying in Singapore over the prolonged period also increased the cost of living for Malaysian work permit holders. Partly due to the pandemic, rental costs had risen by more than 10 per cent for HDB and private apartments (Ng 2022).

RENEWED HOPES

By the final months of 2021, however, with the gradually receding tide of infections on both sides of the border, efforts to re-enable cross-border travel between both sides emerged again with the creation of Vaccinated Travel Lanes (VTLs). This was put in place by the Singapore government with selected countries on account of their ability to control infections within their borders. The Singapore-Malaysia land border was eventually open for travellers on both sides on the 29 November 2021. If one does not take into account the short-lived PCA and RGL agreements that were attempted in 2020, the land borders had been closed to the general public of both Singapore and Malaysia for a total of 621 days.

The VTL between Singapore and Malaysia was part of a broader effort at re-establishing bilateral international travel. At this stage, the re-opening was only made available for returning Malaysians and Singaporeans back to their home country under somewhat limited conditions. The number allowed was limited to 1,440 travellers from either side of the border per day, via 32 consecutive buses operated by private bus operators from both countries (Gov.sg. undated). Needless to say, travellers from either country had to undergo either PCR or ART tests not more than three days before travel to ensure that they were not infected with COVID-19. This is followed up by another test upon arrival at the other side of the border to re-confirm the earlier negative results. Tickets had to be purchased weeks beforehand online while priority was given to returning citizens travelling back to their home country.

In spite of such promising developments, the social and psychological costs of the border closure had already exacted their toll on both Malaysians and Singaporeans cautious about such developments due to fears that another COVID-19 variant would emerge. Such concerns would actually be validated again with the emergence of a new variant known as Omicron in December 2021. This caused both the Singaporean and the Malaysian governments to largely backpedal on the VTL agreement, fearing that a new surge in infections would create new infrastructural problems. This once more created new uncertainty for the following months.

Although initial reports have suggested the relatively lower severity of the Omicron variant, the two governments decided on the side of caution, despite having achieved arguably high level of vaccinations for their respective populations. As the pandemic entered its third year in 2022, there appeared to be some encouraging signs of how the so-called "new normal" would be receding. By February 2022, it was increasingly apparent that the Omicron variant was fortunately not as severe as the Delta variant, despite being more easily spread. Attempts to move ahead in forging a "new normal" of living with the virus eventually led to announcements on 24 March 2022 that the causeways would be accessible from 1 April 2023 for fully vaccinated residents on either side of the border without the need for quarantine nor testing.

FUTURE MOBILITIES IN A POST-COVID-19 WORLD

So, what are the lessons that have been learnt from over two years of separation? It certainly goes without saying that the closure of the two causeways that connected Singapore and Peninsula Malaysia greatly affected the lives of persons on both sides of the border. Apart from the obvious impact on the respective economies of each country, one also needs to take into consideration the social costs of the border lockdown due to the separation of families and all manner of kin. Evidently, scholarly dialogue on the impact of the pandemic on Singapore-Johor Bahru ties needs to take into account its impact on social and emotional well-being. Statistics by the end of 2021 reveal that suicide rates (Hazlin 2021) and domestic violence (Tan 2021) in both countries have risen sharply, revealing a correlation between the pandemic-related lockdowns and social problems. In addition, it is also useful to recall how fertility in both societies have fallen further (Ng 2023 and Zukifli 2021) as a result of the pandemic, hastening the rate of their ageing populations, particularly in the case of Singapore.

Such developments over the two-year border shutdown suggests just how the social, emotional and psychological well-being of many residents on both sides of the border are dependent on such transborder ties. While policymakers and politicians have correctly recognized the significant economic and labour-related dependencies between Singapore and Johor Bahru, what also needs to be taken into consideration are ties that transcend categories of nationality and ethnicity. This is especially so in a world where both globalization and trans-localities increasingly reveal a "post-place" experience of identity and belonging. More specifically, the lived spaces of the urban landscapes of Singapore and Johor Bahru share many overlapping realities and interdependencies that are not easy to separate. Consequently, extended border lockdowns in the face of future pandemics or similar challenges[9] are unlikely to be sustainable in the long-term due to its devastating impact on community and economy. The obvious question here, therefore, is what if a similar crisis were to arise again? With COVID-19 being viewed as "endemic" by both sides at the time of writing, this change in policy mindset has hopefully paved the way for a less reactive but more proactive approach to pandemic management.

In the face of similar scenarios that might once again threaten the relationship between the two cities, it is important that alternative and sustainable solutions need to be explored and created. Perhaps one way forward is to put in place a system that acknowledges the thousands on either side of the border who possess strong familial and socio-economic ties, thus preventing a repeat of the social and psychological toll in future. This is because in our highly globalized world today, the idea of home is not necessarily defined within a single location, because no country is simply an island that is closed off from the rest of the world. From such a vantage point, future policies pertaining to travel between Singapore and Johor Bahru may need to take into account the following categories of ties that link citizens on both sides of the border. They are in the dimensions of *Familial Ties*, *Home Ownership* and *Employment*. These three dimensions stand out as they have been consistently reflected in the challenges and issues that have emerged due to the border closures.

Moving beyond the fallout resulting from the COVID-19 pandemic, it becomes crucial for policymakers to acknowledge and respond with necessary measures to address these three dimensions in the face of future pandemic-like crises in the future. Firstly, it is important to recognize the extent of the nature of familial ties that transcend the land borders that separate Singapore from Johor Bahru. Priority for cross-border commute for persons to gain access to family members seems to be a reasonable arrangement together with other safety measures in place. While not a perfect response to the reality of how such ties can also extend beyond Johor Bahru in Malaysia, this can very much play a significant role in reducing the social and emotional costs for extended separation between the two countries. And although a vast number of the Malaysians who commute daily to Singapore do live in Johor Bahru, many Singaporeans who similarly do so the other way around often have family ties in Johor Bahru and beyond (Chee 2020).

This brings us to the second dimension of home ownership that extends beyond borders. It goes without saying at this point that the existence of familial ties across both sides of the border often results in persons who may choose to live on one side while working on the other. As noted earlier, an estimated number of up to 5,000 (Tan 2016) (or more, just prior to the pandemic) Singaporean families live in Johor Bahru, making up a significant community. The border closure since March 2020 has led to serious disruptions to their everyday lives, often akin to losing one's home virtually overnight. In the case of either Singaporean or Malaysian families who did not possess reliable networks of persons who could assist in looking after their homes in Johor Bahru, there have been disturbing reports of how their homes have been burgled, ransacked and occupied illegally (Ong 2020). In order to address and hopefully minimize such cases, this seems to further justify the need for reasonable but limited access across the Causeway for persons who own homes on the opposite side of where they may be employed.

Finally, the third dimension of employment articulates best, just how economically and social-culturally symbiotic the relationship between Singapore and Johor Bahru has become in recent decades. It should not only take into account the thousands of Malaysians who either live and work in Singapore or the massive numbers from Johor Bahru that traverse the Causeways bi-directionally daily on weekdays to make ends meet, but also the equally numerous Singaporeans who see Johor Bahru as a viable place for a respite from the economic and emotional pressures in their "first-world" nation-state. Although far fewer, there are also a number of Singaporeans who are employed in Malaysia, but details are largely anecdotal (Yong 2013). Nonetheless, all this suggests a well-grounded sense of occupational and commercial ties that were greatly devastated by the border closure. It is useful to recall that up to half of the Malaysian workforce that served as the backbone of many industries in Singapore were lost during the pandemic (Lim 2021). A key lesson learnt from such challenges is how the practice of policies such as the RGL, PCA or the subsequent VTL system needs to be in place earlier in the face of similar limitations on cross-border travel. While the social and economic precarity of Malaysian workers from Johor Bahru have been discussed, it is also important to recognize the corresponding dependency of Singaporeans on them for their skills and labour for essential services that many no longer are capable of or are keen to perform.

Even in the face of a so-called "new normal" due to the COVID-19 coronavirus, perhaps it is important to realize that there is nothing normal (Tan 2020) about it in face of such old ties. Nor should pandemics be used as easy justification to further stoke fears and unjustified resistance towards the relevance of global migrant labour (*The Economist* 2020). Hence, lockdowns and border closures may very well be an important initial strategy in responding to pandemics, but the larger question is whether such measures are sustainable in the long run over periods of a year or more, in light of the deep social bonds fostered along the borderlands between nation-states that share cultural and historical realities. Recalling the recent revival of the project between both governments in the construction of a Rapid Transit System (RTS) that intends to reduce transit time across the border, there appears to be much at stake if a similar crisis occurs. At the time of writing, while the pandemic appears to be receding, its unpredictability remains. While it is undeniably important to ensure the well-being of citizens on either side of the border, ensuring such protection may also have its unforeseen costs. This is especially so when measures to sustain life is ensured ironically at the expense of living, because the Singapore-Johor Bahru link is an indispensable part of life for many.

NOTES

1. At the time of writing, this Facebook group consists of more than 170,000 members. They can be found at https://www.facebook.com/groups/malaysia.singapore.border.crossers.
2. MRT stands for Mass Rapid Transit, Singapore's major provider of rail transport throughout most of the island.
3. Migrant labour in Singapore is divided into two broad groups: the skilled professionals holding an S-pass or E-pass, and the lower-wage contract workers holding a work permit.
4. "Department of Statistics Malaysia Official Portal", www.dosm.gov.my (accessed 6 April 2023).
5. "What Should You Know About Buying Property in Malaysia?" https://www.propertyguru.com.sg/property-guides/buy-property-in-malaysia-17706 (accessed 6 April 2023).
6. At the time of writing, the MMSH programme has been suspended until further notice since July 2020 due to the COVID-19 pandemic. See Amir (2021b).
7. Hello Kitty Town eventually ceased operations on 31 December 2019.
8. Over the last two to three decades, Johor Bahru has also built a reputation as an alternative site for sex tourism among Singaporeans. See *Free Malaysia Today* (2017).
9. More recently, there have been reports of the growing spread of the Monkeypox virus. See Howard and Nedelman (2022).

REFERENCES

Amir Yusof. 2021a. "Putting Dreams on Hold: Young Singaporean Relocates to JB to Care for Grandparents as COVID-19 Shuts Border". *Channel NewsAsia*, 12 May 2021. https://www.channelnewsasia.com/asia/malaysia-singaporeans-johor-bahru-hari-raya-border-closure-mco-1361211.

———. 2021b. "In Focus: How Johor's Residential Property Market has been Hit Hard by COVID-19". *Channel NewsAsia*, 12 June 2021. https://www.channelnewsasia.com/asia/covid19-johor-selling-condo-property-market-malaysia-1838926.

Awang, Azman, Mahbob Salim, and John F. Halldane, eds. 1998. "Indonesia-Malaysia-Singapore Growth Triangle: Borderless Region for Sustainable Progress". *Urban Habitat and Highrise Monograph SEACEUM*. Kuala Lumpur: Institute Sultan Iskandar of Urban Habitat and Highrise.

Baker, Jim. 2014. *Crossroads: A Popular History of Malaysia and Singapore*. Singapore: Marshall Cavendish International.

Bastide, Loïs. 2015. "Faith and Uncertainty: Migrants' Journeys between Indonesia, Malaysia and Singapore". *Health, Risk & Society* 17, nos. 3–4: 226–45.

Chan, Yuk Wah and Brantly Womack. 2016. "Not Merely a Border: Borderland Governance, Development and Transborder Relations in Asia". In *Borderlands in East and Southeast Asia: Emergent Conditions, Relations and Prototypes*, edited by Yuk Wah Chan and Brantly Womack, pp. 93–105. New York and Oxford: Routledge.

Channel NewsAsia. 2018. "Malaysia Floats Plan for Third Link to Singapore", 30 August 2018. https://www.channelnewsasia.com/asia/johor-government-third-link-singapore-bridge-pulau-ubin-807126.

Chee, Glen Juan Jeng. 2020. "Start Singapore-Johor Family Lane So that I Can See My Wife Again". *Today*, 2 September 2020. https://www.todayonline.com/voices/start-singapore-johor-family-lane-so-i-can-see-my-wife-again.

Chia, Osmond. 2021. "Singapore 'Optimistic' that Land Border with Malaysia can Reopen end-Nov, says Covid-19 Task Force". *The Straits Times*, 20 November 2021. https://www.straitstimes.com/singapore/transport/spore-optimistic-that-land-vtl-with-malaysia-can-launch-end-nov-gan-kim-yong.

Chong, Terence, Lee Hock Guan, Norshahril Saat, and Serina Rahman. 2017. *The 2017 Johor Survey: Selected Findings*. Trends in Southeast Asia, no. 20/2017. Singapore: ISEAS – Yusof Ishak Institute.

Chu Mei Mei. 2021. "Malaysia Lifts Travel Restrictions for Fully Vaccinated People". *Reuters*, 10 October 2021. https://www.reuters.com/world/asia-pacific/malaysia-lifts-travel-restrictions-fully-vaccinated-people-2021-10-10/.

Chua, Alvin. 2009. "The Causeway". Singapore Infopedia. https://eresources.nlb.gov.sg/infopedia/articles/SIP_99_2004-12-30.html.

Economist, The. 2020. "When Covid-19 Recedes, Will Global Migration Start Again", 1 August 2020. https://www.economist.com/international/2020/08/01/when-covid-19-recedes-will-global-migration-start-again.

Free Malaysia Today. 2017. "Singapore 'Uncles' Flocking to JB for Fun with Hookers", 17 July 2017. https://www.freemalaysiatoday.com/category/nation/2017/07/17/singaporean-uncles-flocking-to-jb-for-fun-with-hookers/.

Gov.sg. Undated. "Vaccinated Travel Lane (Land) between Singapore and Malaysia". https://www.gov.sg/article/vaccinated-travel-lane-between-singapore-and-malaysia.

Hadi Azmi and Zam Yusa. 2020. "Malaysia: COVID-19 Puts Scrutiny on Tablighi Jamaat". *Benar News.* https://www.benarnews.org/english/news/malaysian/conservative-group-03202020181010.html.

Hampton, Mark P. 2010. "Enclaves and Ethnic Ties: The Local Impacts of Singaporean Cross-border Tourism in Malaysia and Indonesia". *Singapore Journal of Topical Geography* 31: 239–53.

Hazlin Hassan. 2021. "Malaysia sees Rise in Suicides and Calls to Helplines amid Covid-19 Pandemic". *The Straits Times*, 12 July 2021. https://www.straitstimes.com/asia/se-asia/malaysia-sees-rise-in-suicides-and-calls-to-helplines-amid-covid-19-pandemic.

Hodgson, Frances. 2011. "Structures of Encounterability: Space, Place, Paths and Identity". In *Mobilities: New Perspectives in Transport and Society*, edited by Margaret Grieco and John Urry, pp. 41–64. Surrey, UK: Ashgate Publishing Limited.

Howard, Jacqueline and Michael Nedelman. 2022. "Silent Spread of Monkeypox May be a Wakeup Call for the World". *CNN*, 3 June 2022. https://www.cnn.com/2022/06/02/health/monkeypox-endemic-silent-spread/index.html.

Hutchinson, Francis E. and Serina Rahman, eds. 2020. *Johor: Abode of Development?* Singapore: ISEAS – Yusof Ishak Institute.

Koh, Sin Yee. 2015. "How and Why Race Matters: Malaysian-Chinese Transnational Migrants Interpreting and Practising Bumiputera-differentiated Citizenship". *Journal of Ethnic and Migration Studies* 41, no. 3: 531–50.

Kurki, Tuulikki. 2014. "Borders from the Cultural Point of View: An Introduction to Writing at Borders". *Culture Unbound: Journal of Current Cultural Research* 6: 1055–70.

Larsen, Jonas, John Urry, and Kay Axhausen. 2006. *Mobilities, Networks, Geographies.* Hampshire, UK and Burlington, USA: Ashgate Publishing.

Lay, Belmont. 2022. "Hundreds of Thousands of M'sians work in S'pore due to Salary, Stronger Currency, Opportunities & Lifestyle". *Mothership*, 4 July 2022. https://mothership.sg/2022/07/why-malaysians-work-in-singapore-long-term/.

Lim, Ida. 2020. "UN Data shows Malaysians make up Biggest Migrant Group in Singapore at 44pc". *Malay Mail*, 19 January 2020. https://www.malaymail.

com/news/malaysia/2020/01/19/un-data-shows-malaysians-make-up-biggest-migrant-group-in-singapore-at-44pc/1829498.

Lim, John. 2018. "Malaysian Working in Singapore Reveals The Daily Struggles He Goes Through Just For Work". *SAYS*, 2 July 2018. https://says.com/my/news/malaysian-working-in-singapore-shares-hectic-schedule.

Lim, Joyce. 2021. "Only 50% of Malaysian Workers have Returned since Border Reopening". *The Straits Times*, 24 January 2021. https://www.straitstimes.com/business/economy/only-50-of-malaysian-workers-have-returned-since-border-reopening.

———. 2023. "Record-high HDB Rents Driving Malaysians Working in S'pore to Live in JB". *The Straits Times*, 22 January 2023. https://www.straitstimes.com/business/property/record-high-hdb-rents-driving-malaysians-working-in-s-pore-to-live-in-jb.

Lim Tin Seng. 2020. "Malaysia-Singapore Second Link". Singapore Infopedia. https://eresources.nlb.gov.sg/infopedia/articles/SIP_844_2005-01-07.html?s=tuas%20second%20link.

Little, Charles. 2013. "'Hamlet without the Prince': Understanding Singapore-Malaysian Relations through Football". *Soccer & Society* 14, no. 5: 635–51.

Loh, Dylan. 2021. "Singapore's Foreign Population Dips 10.7% on COVID Restrictions". *Nikkei Asia*, 28 September 2021. https://asia.nikkei.com/Politics/Singapore-s-foreign-population-dips-10.7-on-COVID-restrictions.

Nabilah Awang. 2020. "With No Place to Stay, Some Malaysian Workers Sleeping Rough near Kranji MRT Station". *Today*, 19 March 2020. https://www.todayonline.com/singapore/no-place-stay-some-malaysian-workers-sleeping-rough-near-kranji-mrt-station.

Nasongkhla, Sirima and Sidh Sintusingha. 2013. "Social Production of Space in Johor Bahru". *Urban Studies* 50, no. 9: 1836–53.

Ng, Abigail. 2023. "Singapore's Total Fertility Rate Drops to Historic Low of 1.05". *Channel NewsAsia*, 24 February 2023. https://www.channelnewsasia.com/singapore/singapore-total-fertility-rate-population-births-ageing-parentschildren-3301846.

Ng, Michelle. 2022. "Condo, HDB Rents Jump More than 10% in 2021; Demand Slips in December due to Seasonal Lull". *The Straits Times*, 12 January 2022. https://www.straitstimes.com/business/property/condo-hdb-rents-jump-more-than-10-in-2021-demand-slips-in-december-due-to-seasonal-lull.

Ong, Justin and Amir Yusof. 2018. "Clearing the Causeway: Johor Pledges Smoother Journey By Any Means Necessary". *Channel NewsAsia*, 9 June 2018. https://www.channelnewsasia.com/asia/causeway-johor-bahru-commute-second-link-816491.

Ong, Tanya. 2020. "Couple Working in S'pore had M'sia House Broken into & Ransacked, Burglars Allegedly Stayed for Days". *Mothership*, 19 October 2020. https://mothership.sg/2020/10/msia-robbery-house/.

———. 2020. "20 M'sian Families Wave from Yacht to Loved Ones Gathered at Woodlands Park". *Mothership*, 24 October 2020. https://mothership.sg/2020/10/jb-yacht-malaysians-wave.

Rahman, Serina. 2021. "Borderland without Business: The Economic Impact of Covid-19 on Peninsular Malaysia's Southernmost State of Johor". *Fulcrum*, 21 May 2021. Singapore: ISEAS – Yusof Ishak Institute.

Razak, Muhammad Rafeq, Foziah Johar, and Rabiatul Adawiyah Abd Khalil. 2016. "The Impact of Iskandar Malaysia Development on Urban Amenities". *Planning Malaysia: Journal of the Malaysian Institute of Planners*, Special Issue 4: 121–34.

Rizzo, Agatino and Shahed Khan. 2013. "Johor Bahru's Response to Transnational and National Influences in the Emerging Straits Mega-City Region". *Habitat International* 40: 154–62.

Shiraishi, Takashi, ed. 2008. *Across the Causeway: A Multi-Dimensional Study of Malaysia-Singapore Relations*. Singapore: ISEAS – Yusof Ishak Institute.

Straits Times, The. 2017. "Many Malaysians Prefer Working in Singapore for Higher Wages", 31 August 2017. https://www.straitstimes.com/asia/se-asia/many-malaysians-prefer-working-in-singapore-for-higher-wages.

Tai, Janice and Toh Yong Chuan. 2015. "Singaporeans Sick and Elderly Pack Johor Bahru Nursing Homes". *The Straits Times*, 15 March 2015. https://www.straitstimes.com/singapore/health/singaporeans-sick-and-elderly-pack-johor-bahru-nursing-homes.

Tan Boon Hun. Undated. "Some Businesses are Happy as M'sian Workers Come Back to S'pore to Work". Goody Feed. https://goodyfeed.com/businesses-happy-msians-returning.

Tan, Kevin S.Y. 2020. "Singapore-JB ties: Nothing Normal about the New Normal". *Malaysiakini*, 12 June 2020. https://www.malaysiakini.com/letters/529892.

Tan, Lynn. 2016. "About 5,000 Singaporean Families have Set up Home in Johor". *AsiaOne*, 28 May 2016. https://www.asiaone.com/singapore/about-5000-singaporean-families-have-set-home-johor.

Tan, Theresa. 2021. "Family Violence Cases on the Rise in S'pore amid Covid-19 Pandemic". *The Straits Times*, 11 October 2021. https://www.straitstimes.com/singapore/community/family-violence-cases-on-the-rise-in-spore-amid-covid-19-pandemic.

TCW2. 2014. "Malaysians Form the Largest Group of Work Permit Holders by Nationality", 20 March 2014. https://twc2.org.sg/2014/03/20/malaysians-form-the-largest-group-of-work-permit-holders/.

Tho Xin Yi. 2020. "Undaunted by COVID-19 and Border Controls, Malaysian Mums in Singapore Send Around 3,000kg of Breast Milk to Babies Back Home". *Channel NewsAsia*, 21 April 2020. https://www.channelnewsasia.

com/asia/malaysian-covid-19-mums-babies-breast-milk-singapore-deliver-765616.

Today. 2016. "Hard Work Pays off Better in Singapore, say Malaysian Odd Job Workers", 29 February 2016. https://www.todayonline.com/world/asia/hard-work-pays-better-across-causeway-say-malaysian-odd-job-workers.

Urry, John. 2007. *Mobilities*. Cambridge, UK and Malden, USA: Polity Press.

Yang, Calvin. 2016. "Johor's EduCity Drawing Singaporean Students". *AsiaOne*, 11 May 2016. https://www.asiaone.com/singapore/johors-educity-drawing-singaporean-students.

Yang, Hui, Peidong Yang, and Shaohua Zhan. 2017. "Immigration, Population and Foreign Workforce in Singapore: An Overview of Trends, Politics and Issues". *Humanities and Social Science Education Online* 6, no. 1: 10–25.

Yang, Wong. 2020. "Coronavirus: Some Malaysians in Limbo over Their Job Status in Singapore". *The Straits Times*, 22 May 2020. https://www.straitstimes.com/singapore/coronavirus-some-malaysians-in-limbo-over-their-job-status-here.

Ye, Junjia. 2016. "Commuting to Singapore: Johorean Malaysians". In *Class Inequality in the Global City: Global Diversities*. London: Palgrave Macmillan.

Yong, Clement, Jean Iau, and Melissa Heng, 2020. "Coronavirus: Empty Checkpoints at Woodlands, Tuas as Malaysia Lockdown Kicks in". *The Straits Times*, 18 March 2020. https://www.straitstimes.com/singapore/traffic-clears-out-at-woodlands-tuas-checkpoints-as-malaysia-lockdown-kicks-in.

Yong Yan Nie. 2013. "Going the Other Way: Some Singaporeans Thrive in Malaysia". *The Straits Times*, 27 May 2013. https://www.straitstimes.com/singapore/going-the-other-way-some-singaporeans-thrive-in-malaysia.

United Nations. 2019. "International Migrant Stock 2019". Population Division, Department of Economics and Social Affairs, United Nations. https://www.un.org/en/development/desa/population/migration/data/estimates2/estimates19.asp.

United Nations Department of Economic and Social Affairs. Undated. "Migration Profiles: Singapore". https://esa.un.org/miggmgprofiles/indicators/files/Singapore.pdf.

Wong, Kayla. 2020. "S'pore to provide S$50 per night for 14 nights to firms for each worker affected by M'sia lockdown". *Mothership*, 17 March 2020. https://mothership.sg/2020/03/malaysian-workers-50/.

Zazali Musa. 2005. "JB City Square a Pride of 2 Nations". *The Star*, 15 August 2005. https://www.thestar.com.my/business/business-news/2005/08/15/jb-city-square-a-pride-of-2-nations.

Zukifli, Ahmad Mustakim. 2021. "Birth Rate Drops to Lowest in Decades amid Pandemic". *Malaysia Now*, 14 October 2021. https://www.malaysianow.com/news/2021/10/14/birth-rate-drops-to-lowest-in-decades-amid-pandemic.

4

UNEQUAL FLOWS: EXAMINING THE FACTORS SURROUNDING THAI AND VIETNAMESE LABOUR MIGRATION TO SOUTH KOREA

Steve K.L. CHAN

INTRODUCTION

Globalization often implies the increased flow of persons, goods and information across country borders. Consequently, labour migration between Southeast Asia and the rest of Asia is part of this trend. This is a unique phenomenon unlike migrant flows between the emerging economies of Asia and developed Western countries. This chapter, therefore, examines the reasons and policy issues surrounding the movement of unskilled migrant workers from Thailand and Vietnam to South Korea. The two countries are of great interest in this regard as they are two of the fastest ageing societies in Southeast Asia, with Vietnam having the youngest population in the region. But demographic numbers on fertility and mortality do not tell the full story, as it is important to examine the role of policies adopted by each country with South Korea's Employment Permit System (EPS), in influencing such flows. The reasons and patterns for such migration are based on empirical data drawn from field observations and interviews.

METHODOLOGY

The purpose of this study is to uncover the reasons surrounding the outgoing movement of unskilled migrant workers from Thailand and Vietnam to South Korea, and its impact on population change at the source of migrants. Therefore, the relationship of South Korea's EPS to such migration flows will be examined. This study entailed qualitative research consisting of key informant interviews and archival research. The key informant interviews were conducted in Seoul, Bangkok and Daegu. A Korean labour union, women's NGO, Thai labour migrant NGO as well as one Thai and one Vietnamese migrant worker were interviewed in 2018 and 2019. These interviews enabled the author to examine the situation of documented and undocumented workers in South Korea and the roles that migration intermediaries play in the process. All the interviews were conducted anonymously. For the archival research, censuses and labour migration reports of South Korea, Vietnam and Thailand were reviewed.

REASONS FOR LABOUR MIGRATION

Existing migration theories seldom address the transnational movement of labour in connection to demographic factors. At a glance, developing countries with young populations tend to export their excess labour force. Classical push-pull discourse claims that labour surplus in the sending country and labour deficit at the destination trigger the flow in both ways (Lee 1966; Castles and Miller 2009). A younger labour force, which means an abundant supply of labour, in the sending origins is a "push" factor for migrants, while an ageing society and shrinking labour force in South Korea is a "pull" factor. However, neo-classical theory places more emphasis on economic factors to explain the move. Apart from jobs, political instability, backwardness, and natural disaster are also push factors. For example, the deprivation of citizenship has triggered the outflow of ethnic minorities from Myanmar to Thailand (Chan 2018). Geographical wage disparity also reinforces labour migration flows from low-wage to high-wage areas. Besides wage differentials, families may consider risk control and diversifying the allocation of resources for the move (Stark 1991; Massey et al. 2008).

Migration is usually not the decision of individuals; network theory concerns the role of the family and community in the migration process, from decision-making, funding the journey, job seeking, and residential choice, to remittance, all retaining ties to home. Migration is an ongoing process through the use of these networks. Migrant networks draw individuals into co-ethnic settlements and enable the formation of migrant communities at the destination. Immigration enclaves draw new arrivals into these neighbourhoods, which facilitate the formation of co-ethnic social and economic infrastructure, including associations, clubs, grocery shops, restaurants, and the like (Portes and Manning 1986; Chan 2015). Existing studies have examined many such enclaves, including Chinatown in New York (Zhou 1992), Koreatown in Los Angeles (Zhou and Cho 2010), a Thai community at Singapore's Golden Mile Complex (Tan 2018), trading hubs of mobile phones and IT products of Africans at Chungking Mansions in Hong Kong (Mathews 2011).

Whether the move is temporary or permanent, migrants tend to stay in touch with their place of origin. The flow of information, exchange of ideas and cooperation creates a social space across country borders. Transnationalism, which concerns the activities linking back to the sending countries and the interaction between the emigrants, prospective migrants, returnees and other people remaining in the sending countries, has become a topic in migration studies in recent decades. The social space enhances different communities that exist in-between the origin and the destination. Such a perspective examines connections between places and peoples, the meanings and impacts on identities, habitus, actions and structures (Faist 2010). These mobile individuals and communities live "dual lives" who speak their own native language and that of the host society, and view both the sending and receiving ends as "home" (Portes et al. 1999).

At the same time, the role of intermediaries throughout the migration process should not be ignored. A migrant broker is a middleman who provides services, usually for a fee, to facilitate the migration.

An official broker is a licensed agent who works with governments of sending and/or receiving countries and migrants. Whether licensed or not, many are commercial brokers who take part in the migration process for profit where the commercialization of these migration agents is no longer limited to smuggling or negative aspects of their services (Spaan and Hillmann 2013). They are either a sizeable company or individual returnees who work for the employers in receiving countries to recruit prospective migrant workers (Sakaew and Tangpratchakoon 2009). These intermediaries actualize the move by brokering desires, reducing uncertainty, matching employers and job-seekers and provide material services (Chan 2022).

Massey et al. (2008) consider the complexity of international migration, which is not only motivated by wage disparity or economic reasons, but includes various factors that "perpetuate itself across time and space" (p. 42). The idea of cumulative causation suggests that once the first migration event happens, the social context within the sending origin will change, which contributes to continued and further emigration (Massey 1990). Eight factors are identified by Massey et al. (2008) as contributing to sustained migration flows over time, namely:

1. The expansion of migration networks reaching a critical threshold;
2. The distribution of income among their reference group;
3. The distribution of land, especially relating to farmland purchase at the migrants' hometowns;
4. The trend for industrial farming leading to the displacement of agrarian labour;
5. The culture of migration at the point of origin, which encourages out-migration;
6. The depletion of human capital in the origin communities and accumulation at the destinations, enhancing the outflow of migrants;
7. The stigmatization of "immigrant jobs" making local workers less keen on them; and
8. The structure of production (pp. 46–48).

The discourse of the cumulative causation of labour migration summarizes a variety of reasons for the perpetuation of the migration movement. One agrees that a single reason is insufficient in explaining the current patterns of migration among workers from Southeast Asian countries to South Korea. However, the aforementioned eight factors do not include demography. When examining labour migration patterns in South Korea and their countries of origin, the ageing population in South Korea is a draw, and conversely, the younger labour force of Vietnam should be a pushing force for the emigration of its migrant workers. But the ageing hypothesis does not explain the migration flow of Thai labour to South Korea well, because the population of Thailand is no longer young, though not the oldest in the region. Notestein's (1945, c.f. Notestein 1983) demographic transition theory uses the change in birth and death rates in different stages of economic development to predict population growth.[1] The economy of South Korea is, no doubt the most mature, and Vietnam should remain in the early industrialization period, with Thailand situated in-between. The proposed model for this chapter, therefore, explains the existing differentiation in population and ageing among the three societies. It is important to build a framework of cumulative causation in relation to demographic transition to determine labour migration patterns. The findings fill the knowledge gap in better understanding cumulative causation and ageing societies in the context of Northeast Asia and Southeast Asia labour migration patterns.

DEMOGRAPHIC DIFFERENCES

The aforementioned population transition model helps to explain how South Korea, Thailand and Vietnam fall along a continuum of population characteristics by age, with South Korea being the oldest on average, Vietnam the youngest, and Thailand in between. The median age of Koreans was 43.1 years in 2018—0.7 years higher than in 2017 (42.4 years). There was a year-on-year drop in the youth population aged 0–14 and the working-age population aged 15–64. On the other hand, there was a year-on-year rise in the population aged 65 or more (Statistics Korea 2019). With a low fertility rate, the trend of population growth will continue to be flattened with a projected negative growth of –0.12 per cent in 2035 (Statistics Korea 2017).

The nature of its ageing population suggests that South Korea is an emigration society. Foreign nationals in South Korea amounted to

1.65 million persons in 2018, or 3.2 per cent of the total population. This figure increased by 170,000 persons (or 11.6 per cent) from 1.48 million persons in 2017. As for foreigners by nationality, Chinese nationals (including Korean-Chinese) constituted the largest foreign national group, with a population of 760,000 persons (or 46 per cent of the total foreign population). For Korean-Chinese known as *Joseonjok* (in Korean: 조선족) who are Chinese migrants of Korean and PRC Chinese descent, the ethnic closeness and geographic proximity respectively favour the flow. There were about 530,000 Korean-Chinese and 220,000 PRC Chinese (or 32.2 per cent and 13 per cent of the total foreign nationals respectively). Compared to 2017 figures, it was Thai nationals that recorded the highest increase (58,000 persons), followed by the Korean-Chinese (34,000 persons). As expected, most of them are located in Seoul, the capital city, and the surrounding Gyeonggi-do Province, as well as Gyeongnam Province, where the second-largest city, Busan, is located.

Vietnam and Thailand were the two main sources of inward labour migration. More than one-third of Vietnam's growing 98 million population is below 25 years old, making it one of the youngest populations in Asia, with a median age of 31.9 years. Thailand has more people below 25 years old compared to people over 55 years old, but the sizes of these two groups are growing closer. The median age of Thailand was 39 years old, in-between South Korea and Vietnam (CIA undated).

TABLE 4.1
Age Structure of South Korea, Vietnam and Thailand

Age group	Korea	Thailand	Vietnam
0–14 years	12.8%	16.5%	22.6%
15–24 years	11.2%	13.0%	15.2%
25–54 years	44.6%	45.7%	45.7%
55–64 years	15.5%	13.0%	9.6%
65 years & above	15.9%	11.8%	6.9%
Total population	51,835,110	68,977,400	98,721,275

Source: Data from *The World Factbook* (CIA undated).

EMPLOYMENT PERMIT SYSTEM OF SOUTH KOREA

Korea is a medium-sized country with an ageing population. The relatively mature economy consists of primary production (3.8 per cent), manufacturing (17.6 per cent), construction (7.8 per cent), trading, accommodation and food (23.1 per cent), electricity, transport, communication and finance (11.8 per cent), as well as business, service and others (37.1 per cent) (Statistics Korea 2019). Similar to other developed nations around the globe, the country's industrial structure shows a growing tertiary sector and contracting manufacturing and agriculture sectors. Local workers are participating less in sectors like construction, manufacturing and farming. A sectorial labour shortage made the South Korean government introduce a trial trainee scheme and subsequently relied on massive imports of foreign labour.

The "Overseas Investment Firm Industrial Trainee System", which was enforced from 1992 to 2006, aimed to provide training for semi-skilled labour from developing countries. It can be viewed as a trial for the import of a small number of unskilled labour migrants from developing countries to complement its aged but high-waged labour force. South Korea is relatively more homogenous than other societies, but there are cultural minorities that are not always apparent. The government hesitated to import foreign labour regardless of the strong demand from labour-intensive sectors in the 1980s. The attempt was controversial as employers were keener on taking advantage of their low wages than providing them on-the-job training. In many cases, the wage and working conditions were unsatisfactory. The Open Working Group on Labor Migration and Recruitment (2014) found that the wage of trainees was low and even lower than that of the undocumented workers. These so-called "trainees" were, in fact, used for labour (Park and Kim 2016). The Trainee System was terminated in 2006 following strong public criticism.

The Employment Permit System (EPS), introduced in 2004 as a replacement for the Trainee System, was a bold step to open up for unskilled foreign workers. The measure was enforced alongside an employment management system, which recruited temporary foreign workers of Korean ancestry (mainly the *Joseonjok*). Besides recruiting foreign labour to fill unskilled and unwanted job vacancies, the EPS also addressed the labour shortage in small-and-medium-sized enterprises that struggled to legally hire low-skilled foreign workers (Park and

Kim 2016). The EPS is based on a Memorandum of Understanding signed by Korea with sixteen labour-sending countries in South and Southeast Asia (Park 2017). A quota of foreign workers was set to make sure workers are allocated into relevant industrial sectors. Foreign workers are granted a work permit for three years, with an extension of one year and ten months, then an additional three-year permit and a one-year-and-ten-month extension. After that, the foreign worker has to return home (Open Working Group on Labor Migration and Recruitment 2014). This is to ensure these unskilled workers cannot attempt to become permanent residents due to reasons of naturalization (Park and Kim 2016). Moreover, the EPS is directly administered by Korean embassies in the labour-sending countries with all intermediaries excluded, but informal brokers are still actively involved and undocumented migrant workers can find loopholes to enter and work in South Korea.

Marriage remains the only way for foreign unskilled workers to seek permanent immigration. In fact, so-called "foreign bride buying" is encouraged in the form of government subsidies for rural men to marry foreign women (Kim 2019). Vietnamese brides are the largest group of international marriages. In general, Vietnamese, Chinese and Thai brides constituted 30 per cent, 21.6 per cent, and 6.6 per cent respectively in 2018 (Kim 2019). It is also important to note that a marriage visa (F6) is different from an employment permit. A migrant worker who is married to a Korean bride may switch to a marriage visa and extend his stay in the country by two years, which is the length of a marriage visa. The requirements for visa renewal are that it has to be renewed bi-annually, and further applying for permanent residency and naturalization makes the foreign bride dependent on her Korean husband, which in some cases, leads to domestic violence issues (Iglauer 2015).

FINDINGS FROM INTERVIEWS

(A) Push and Pull Factors for migration to Korea

The initial findings on the push and pull factors of labour migration shows that the wage differential is a key determinant of labour flows from both Thailand and Vietnam into South Korea. "The wage disparity between Thailand and South Korea has attracted many Thai young workers to South Korea […] Many of these Thais are from rural areas in the provinces where there is less choice of jobs and lower wage", Mr A, a Thai NGO leader confirmed with the author in an interview in Bangkok. Exploring urban life in a developed nation is a draw for labour migrants to South Korea. Surprisingly, Korean popular culture can be a pull factor for labour migration. Mr A further said, "These migrant workers are young people from rural areas of Thailand who want to explore the outside world […] They try their luck for quick money and make a change to their rural life […] The growing popularity of K-pop culture attract them to work in South Korea."

On the other hand in South Korea, domestic employers generally favour migrant workers. They work hard and receive lower wages than locals. The minimum wage was 8,350 Korean won per hour (US$7.37) in 2019. Most (documented) migrant workers get this rate, but the average salary for local workers is much higher.

> "Migrant workers come to make money; they treat the chance for overtime work and night shift as a bonus […] some even want to work seven days a week for earning extra wage […] almost all Koreans resist overtime and weekends duties. Migrant workers also fill up primarily unskilled positions because training needs Korean language skill." – Mr C, a Korean trade union worker in Daegu, highlighted the preference for migrant workers to locals.

At the same time, it was noted that some employers take advantage of undocumented workers. "Undocumented workers get lesser wage […] and hesitate to complain because the employer may threaten to report them to immigration office", Mr C noted. Some employers also do not provide medical insurance to migrant workers, despite it being an EPS requirement. Besides, migrant workers also fill vacancies for jobs that Koreans are unwilling to do, particularly 3Ds jobs (i.e. Dirty, Dangerous and Demeaning). Mr C also noted:

> "The working conditions in this industrial complex are less desirable. Many factories are small subcontractors of large conglomerates (e.g. supplier of Hyundai Motor Company) […] the factories make rubber parts for the vehicles; its petrochemical smells bad. Also, factories using press machines for metal parts hire primarily migrant workers. They are dangerous with a risk of injury to hand or fingers; Korean workers avoid these jobs".

(B) Labour Brokers

The EPS excludes any role of an intermediary in the application process. But these middlemen still find loopholes to provide their services. The author finds that Vietnamese migrant workers largely follow the official EPS procedure; almost all are documented workers at least for the first session of four years and ten months. Some turn to local recruitment agents in Korea if they want to continue their work there without a break back home in Vietnam and to apply through the EPS for another round.

But Thai migrant workers often use informal brokers to enter South Korea and work undocumented. A Thai informant in South Korea told the author that there are more undocumented Thai workers than documented ones in the country. "As far as I know in Daegu, there are only 20,000 documented workers out of 100,000", said Ms B, a Thai migrant worker-turned-NGO worker in a migrant women's service centre in Daegu of South Korea.

Many Thais did not follow the formal EPS channel when applying for an employment permit to enter South Korea. The EPS system limits the industrial sectors eligible to hire foreign workers, and those beyond the list typically turn to undocumented workers. These Thai migrant workers, known as *khon phi* in Thai (literally means "ghost people"), were widely found in designated multicultural zones for foreign industrial workers in South Korea.[2] These Thais did not qualify for the Korean EPS but still tried to fulfill their version of "the Korean dream" (Smutkupt 2014). One of these requirements is knowledge of the Korean language, and migrant workers must pass the Korean proficiency test, which has proved difficult for low-educated migrant workers from Thailand.

> "To apply for an employment permit is hard which requires much money and time [...] the Korean language proficiency requirement is a barrier. They have to attend a Korean language class for six months [part-time] before the application. The tuition fee costs around 30,000 to 40,000 Thai Baht (US$960–1,280). Many failed the first attempt of the proficiency test and need to re-sit again. There are only two rounds of the exam per year." – Ms B.

Intermediaries play a significant role in the migration process in Thailand. They are official recruitment agencies that are licensed by the authorities at both the sending and receiving countries and provide a wide range of services for profit to facilitate labour migration. Many of these brokers are return migrants from South Korea who provide the service informally.

> "I know two to three brokers in my town and nearby who are returnees who worked formerly in South Korea. They remain a connection in South Korea [...] They don't tell the full story to their customers who are the neighbours and villagers here in Thailand [...] They are individuals, not a migration agent company. Some don't identify themselves as a 'broker', but the neighbours of other villagers who give a helping hand [for a stipend] if these people want to work overseas." – Mr A.

Information gaps and hearsay have led these rural youths to use a broker in their village. Such brokers typically channel prospective migrants away from the formal EPS procedure, which excludes intermediaries.

> "Many of these Thai workers are lowly educated, rural people know little about South Korea, working conditions, and no idea of the EPS procedure [...] they rely on their friends and neighbours as the first contact [...] they are drawn into the 'path' towards undocumented labour migration in some cases." – Mr A.

(C) Get Married, Sojourning or Going Back?

Similar to their Thai counterparts, Vietnamese migrant workers are drawn to South Korea primarily due to the wage differential. But Vietnam is a developing economy with fewer job opportunities in the past decade. A relevant case is that of Ms D, a Vietnamese migrant worker and an active participant in the Korean Trade Union's activities. The trade union referred her to be interviewed because she had been working in Korea for ten years and was familiar with the situation and policies implementation on the ground. Starting from a documented worker for the first four-year-and-ten-month period under the EPS, she was reluctant to go back to Vietnam and has been an undocumented worker for the past five years. "There were not many jobs available in Vietnam ten years ago. Many people wanted to work overseas and earn more money", she noted, when explaining why she decided to move to Korea. She has worked in several cities and eight companies in the ten years she has been in the country. She changes her job almost every year because of reasons such as her employer going bankrupt, underpaying her, having bad working conditions, and salary delays. Once, she even witnessed her coworkers being sexually harassed by the boss. As an undocumented worker, she is free to leave her job. But when she was working under the EPS, she had to get the permission of her employer to change jobs, and even this was limited to three job changes, under EPS rules. She speaks conversational Korean now, but does not have Koreans as close friends. As her job is not stable and lacks strong local connections, Ms D is concerned about her future in the country.

> "I struggle to continue staying in South Korea undocumented or going back. There are a growing number of job opportunities now in Vietnam, but the wage level still far from here in Korea [...] And I may not adapt to the environment in my hometown after working ten years in Korea [...] younger generation in Vietnam are more educated, I am no longer young and therefore, not confident to compete a decent job with them [...] I have yet to decide to stay or to return." – Ms D.

In recent years, Vietnam's economy has been growing rapidly. Many multinational corporations are investing in Vietnam. The relatively acceptable wage level of the country has been attracting electronics and manufacturing companies to open or relocate their factories there. These include Samsung, the Korean electronics giant.

In mid-2022, the whole world gradually relaxed border control and distancing measures, signifying post-COVID-19 pandemic normalcy. Migrant workers who have felt isolated and severely affected, especially those who overstayed their visas and work undocumented, may choose to leave South Korea and return to their homes in Thailand and Vietnam.[3] Vietnam will be no doubt keen to encourage their migrant workers from overseas to return home and fill the growing job vacancies. Hence, Ms D is not alone, her dilemma on whether to stay or return home is typical among Vietnamese workers in South Korea.

There exists one more alternative: to get married to a Korean and obtain permanent residency, and subsequently work towards becoming a naturalized Korean citizen. In fact, many migrant workers, primarily female, have taken this route. "Many of these Thais are from the rural areas [...] some are divorced, single mothers looking for a new marriage with a Korean man in order to gain long-stay status in Korea, not only a job", said Mr A.

The South Korean government adopted a multicultural marriage policy as a strategy to address the country's low fertility rate and population ageing. "It's not easy to get along in a multicultural marriage, especially for a rural Korean man married to a Vietnamese bride, because the language barrier, cultural gap, lifestyle difference can be sources of conflict", said Ms E, who heads a migrant women service centre in Daegu. As the importance of the traditional family in the country has changed during postmodern times, there is now a higher divorce rate and more single-parent households.

> "When the transnational marriage emerged in Korea one or two decades ago, it was the first marriage of Korean men and migrant women. But recently, with more and more marriages between divorced families, [...] we noticed that a growing number of migrant women using our counselling services have been victims of sexual and domestic violence."
> – Ms E.

Migrant women are vulnerable and if domestic violence emerges, they are doubly disadvantaged. Under the present immigration policy of South Korea, migrants under a marriage visa must leave the country after divorce. Ms E criticized the existing immigration law and multicultural family policy:

> "The migrant women need to depart Korea when they have divorced, and have even become victims of domestic violence [...] some have also turned into undocumented persons as they fled from their homes [...] others return to their home country with regret upon failing both their marriage and career in South Korea." – Ms E.

DISCUSSION AND CONCLUSION

The initial findings of this research conformed to some well-known, push-pull factors of labour migration, including wage differentials and the duality of the labour market. Also, as South Korea is an ageing society, the labour shortage has drawn younger workers towards it; these include nationals from Vietnam and Thailand, as well as other developing countries.

But the population of Thailand is no longer young and demographic factors are not sufficient in explaining such labour migration patterns. The author argues that cumulative causation, consisting of the aforementioned reasons—exploring urban life, fondness for K-pop culture, desire for transnational marriage, and the like—helps to better describe the whole picture. In addition, the findings from this research suggest two patterns of labour migration, namely, the asymmetry of labour flows between Vietnam and Korea, as well as a chain of labour flows between Korea, Thailand and its neighbors. Figure 4.1 illustrates the combined patterns.

FIGURE 4.1
Combined Pattern of Asymmetric and Chain of Labour Flows

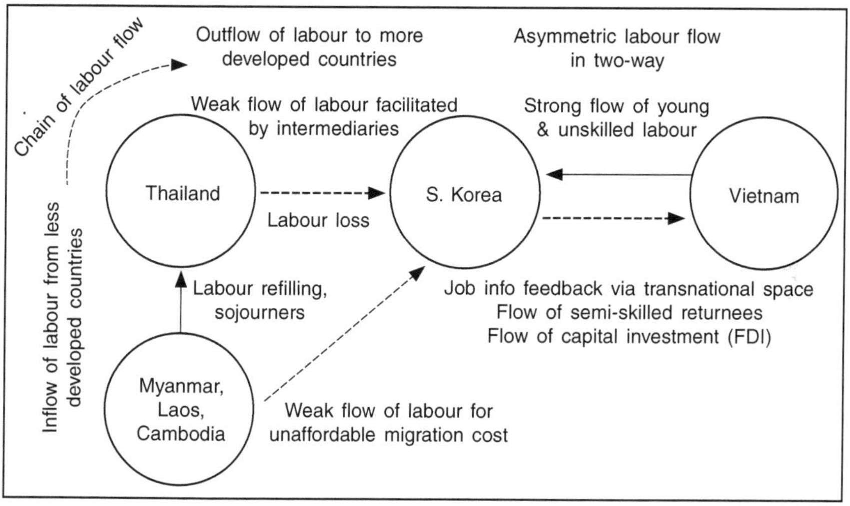

```
                    Outflow of labour to more       Asymmetric labour flow
         Chain of labour flow
                    developed countries                 in two-way

                    Weak flow of labour facilitated   Strong flow of young
                         by intermediaries            & unskilled labour

                    ┌─────────┐                  ┌─────────┐              ┌─────────┐
                    │         │ ──────────────▶  │         │              │         │
                    │ Thailand│                  │ S. Korea│ ◀──────────  │ Vietnam │
 Inflow of labour   │         │   Labour loss    │         │ ──────────▶  │         │
 from less          └─────────┘                  └─────────┘              └─────────┘
 developed                ▲ Labour refilling,     Job info feedback via transnational space
 countries                │ sojourners            Flow of semi-skilled returnees
                    ┌─────────┐                   Flow of capital investment (FDI)
                    │ Myanmar,│
                    │ Laos,   │  Weak flow of labour for
                    │Cambodia │  unaffordable migration cost
                    └─────────┘
```

Source: Author

(i) Asymmetric Labour Flows

Although some migrant workers may settle down and get married to local people in the destination country, many are sojourners and the vast majority of them return to their country of origin upon retirement. The sojourn pattern varies, involving a cycle of documented migration and return (up to the permissible duration of the EPS); a single attempt of documented migration before returning home; becoming an undocumented worker after a documented stint; undocumented thorough one's stay; and finally getting married and settling down permanently.

It is also important to note that migration from Vietnam to South Korea, in some instances, benefits the latter more, with more Korean direct investment and relocation of production plants to Vietnam. Labour migration has also improved mutual understanding between sending and receiving countries. Many Vietnames returnees bring with them working experience with Korean companies, are familiar with the Korean management style, and speak the Korean language. The initial migration and work in Korea has become brokerage between Vietnamese and Korean cultures, which later facilitates the formation of an "asymmetric system" of migration. The Vietnamese returnees, speaking Korean and familiar with Korean management also tend to work in Korean factories in Vietnam.

(ii) A Chain of Labour Flows

The migration trend of Thais to South Korea cannot be more different to the Vietnamese experience. A rapidly ageing Thai society is competing with South Korea for labour. A disparity in wages between the two countries has triggered a weak labour flow outward from Thailand. Informal brokers help to catalyze the movement regardless of the EPS of South Korea, excluding the use of formal intermediaries. Thais typically make use of intermediaries, and both licensed agencies and informal brokers facilitate labour importation from neighbouring countries. Finally, ageing, development and even the labour market (surplus and deficit) are highly related. To compensate for the weak labour outflow (440,000),[4] Thailand needs to draw more labour (about 2.9–4 million)[5] from its relatively less developed neighbours, namely Myanmar, Laos and Cambodia, to compensate for the labour loss. As such, Thailand is benefitting from a net gain of manpower with both a strong inflow and a weak outflow of labour.

NOTES

1. The four stages are: Stage 1—the pre-industrialization period, where both the birth rates and death rates are high, resulting in stable population growth; in Stage 2, there is rapid population growth owing to a high birth rates, but falling death rates; this trend continues in Stage 3, along with decreasing population growth because of falling birth rates and low death rates; in Stage 4, low birth rates and low death rates lead to a stable but low population growth (Notestein 1945, c.f. Notestein 1983).

2. Smutkupt (2014) explains that the phenomenon of *khon phi* is not restricted to Thai migrant workers, but also Vietnamese, Chinese, and undocumented workers from other sending origins.
3. Vietnam declared COVID-19 endemic and reopened the country for international flights from February 2022; COVID-19 testing requirements for all international arrivals were dropped from May 2022. Thailand allowed fully vaccinated Thais and visitors to enter without quarantine and abandoned its "Test & Go" testing regime and one-day hotel waiting (quasi-quarantine) for the result in May 2022.
4. Figure from Ministry of Labour, Thailand in 2018 (Ministry of Labour 2018).
5. Official figure from IMF (2019) showed 2.9 million migrant workers registered in Thailand; but Thai NGOs, like Mekong Migration Networks (MMN), estimated that there were four million migrant workers in Thailand (Chongkittavorn 2020).

REFERENCES

Castles, Stephen and Mark J. Miller. 2009. *The Age of Migration*. New York, N.Y.: Palgrave Macmillan.

Central Intelligence Agency (CIA). Undated. *The World Factbook*. https://www.cia.gov/library/publications/resources/the-world-factbook/.

Chan, Steve Kwok-Leung. 2015. "Segregation Dimensions and Development Differentials of Ethnic Enclave: Thai Restaurants in the Kowloon City of Hong Kong". *International Journal of Social Economics* 42, no. 1: 82–96. https://doi.org/10.1108/IJSE-06-2013-0144.

———. 2018. "Deprivation of Citizenship, Undocumented Labor and Human Trafficking: Myanmar Migrant Workers in Thailand". *Regions and Cohesion* 8, no. 2: 82–106.

———. 2022. "Transnational Brokers and the Desire for Labor Migration: Decision-making Process of Myanmar Migrant Workers in Thailand". *Journal of International Migration and Integration* 23. https://doi.org/10.1007/s12134-021-00915-0.

Chongkittavorn, Kavi. 2020. "Migrant Workers Need Better Welfare". *Bangkok Post*, 22 December 2020. https://www.bangkokpost.com/opinion/opinion/2039215/migrant-workers-need-better-welfare.

Faist, Thomas. 2010. "Diaspora and Transnationalism: What Kind of Dance Partners?" In *Diaspora and Transnationalism: Concepts, Theories and Methods*, edited by Rainer Bauböck and Thomas Faist, pp. 9–34. Amsterdam: Amsterdam University Press.

Iglauer, Philip. 2015. "South Koreas Foreign Bride Problem: The Government Tries to Tackle the Thorny Issue of Migrant Brides and Domestic Violence". *Diplomats*, 29 January 2015. https://thediplomat.com/2015/01/south-koreas-foreign-bride-problem/.

International Labour Organization (ILO). 2019. "TRIANGLE in ASEAN Quarterly Briefing Note", Thailand (July–September 2019). https://www.ilo.org/wcmsp5/groups/public/---asia/---ro-bangkok/documents/genericdocument/wcms_614383.pdf.

Kim, Bo-gyung. 2019. "Encourage Foreign 'Bride Buying': Rural Counties Offer Men Marrying Foreign Brides Money to Defray Costs". *The Korea Herald*, 26 February 2019. http://www.koreaherald.com/view.php?ud=20190218000459.

Kim, Kwang-tae. 2019. "International Marriages in South Korea up 8.5 Percentage in 2018". *Yonhap News Agency*, 6 November 2019. https://en.yna.co.kr/view/AEN20191106005200320.

Lee, Everett S. 1966. "A Theory of Migration". *Demography* 3: 47–57.

Massey, Douglas S. 1990. "Social Structure, Household Strategies, and the Cumulative Causation of Migration". *Population Index* 56: 3–26.

Massey, Douglas S., Joaquin Arango, Graeme Hugo, Ali Kouaouci, Adela Pellegrino, and J. Edward Taylor. 2008. *Worlds in Motion: Understanding International Migration at the End of the Millennium*. Oxford: Oxford University Press.

Mathews, Gordon. 2011. *Ghetto at the Centre of the World: Chungking Mansions*. Chicago: Chicago University Press.

Ministry of Labour, Thailand. 2018. "Gen. Adul" glad Thai Workers in Foreign Countries Make More than 1.2 Billion Baht a Year", 18 May 2018. https://www.mol.go.th/en/news/gen-adul-glad-thai-workers-in-foreign-countries-make-more-than-1-2-billion-baht-a-year-2#:~:text=At%20present%2C%20there%20are%20about,the%20Middle%20East%20and%20Europe.

Notestein, Frank W. 1983. "Frank Notestein on Population Growth and Economic Development". *Population and Development Review* 9, no. 2: 345–60. https://doi.org/10.2307/1973057.

Open Working Group on Labor Migration and Recruitment. 2014. "South Korea's Employment Permit System: A Successful Government-to-Government Model?" *Open Working Group on Labor Migration & Recruitment*, Policy Brief No. 2. http://mfasia.org/migrantforumasia/wp-content/uploads/2015/06/policybrief_epskorea_2015.pdf.

Park, Young-bum. 2017. "South Korea Carefully Tests the Waters on Immigration, With a Focus on Temporary Workers". *Migration Information Source*, 1 March 2017. https://www.migrationpolicy.org/article/south-korea-carefully-tests-waters-immigration-focus-temporary-workers.

Park, Young-bum and Myung-hui Kim. 2016. *Korea's Temporary Low-skilled Foreign Worker Program: Employment Permit System*. Ulsan: Human Resources Development Service of Korea.

Portes, Alejandro and Robert D. Manning. 1986. "The Immigrant Enclave: Theory and Empirical Examples". In *Competitive Ethnic Relations*, edited by Susan Olzak and Joane Nagel, pp. 47–68, Orlando, FL: Academic Press.

Sakaew, Sompong and Patima Tangpratchakoon. 2009. *Brokers and Labor Migration from Myanmar: A Case Study from Samut Sakhon*. Bangkok: The Labor Rights Promotion Network.

Smutkupt, Suriya. 2014. "Being *khon phi* as a Form of Resistance among Thai Migrant Workers in Korea". *Sojourn: Journal of Social Issues in Southeast Asia* 29, no. 3: 721–37.

Spaan, Ernst and Felicitas Hillmann. 2013. "Migration Trajectories and the Migration Industry: Theoretical Reflections and Empirical Examples from Asia". In *The Migration Industry and the Commercialization of International Migration*, edited by Thomas Gammeltoft-Hansen and Ninna Nyberg Sørensen, pp. 64–86. Abingdon, OX: Routledge.

Stark, Oded. 1991. *The Migration of Labor*. Cambridge and Oxford: Blackwell.

Statistics Korea. 2019. "2018 Population and Housing Census". http://kostat.go.kr/portal/eng/pressReleases/8/7/index.board?bmode=read&bSeq=&aSeq=378503&pageNo=1&rowNum=10&navCount=10&currPg=&searchInfo=&sTarget=title&sTxt=.

⸻. 2020. "International Migration Statistics in 2019". https://www.kostat.go.kr/portal/eng/pressReleases/8/5/index.board?bmode=read&bSeq=&aSeq=384167&pageNo=1&rowNum=10&navCount=10&currPg=&searchInfo=&sTarget=title&sTxt=.

Tan, Kevin S.Y. 2018. "Traversing the Golden Mile: An Ethnographic Outline of Singapore's Thai Enclave". *Urbanities* 8, no. 1: 3–19.

Zhou, Min. 1992. *Chinatown: The Socioeconomic Potential of an Urban Enclave*. Philadelphia: Temple University Press.

Zhou, Min and Myungduk Cho. 20101. "Noneconomic Effects of Ethnic Entrepreneurship: A Focused Look at the Chinese and Korean Enclave Economics in Los Angeles". *Thunderbird International Business Review* 52, no. 2: 83–96. https://doi.org/10.1002/tie.20316.

5

EMPLACING MULTICULTURALISM: SOUTHEAST ASIAN MIGRANT LINGUISTIC ACCULTURATION PROGRAMMES AND COMMUNITY BUILDING IN SOUTH KOREA

Ivan V. Small

INTRODUCTION

Over the last generation the Vietnamese migrant population in South Korea has grown significantly and become quite visible. Vietnamese in South Korea number over 170,000 and now count as the largest expatriate population in the country after Chinese (Park 2018). One of the most significant remittance corridors is now South Korea-Vietnam, which has outpaced Overseas Development Assistance (ODA) flows. The majority of Vietnamese in Korea tend to fall into three categories—labour migrants, spouses, and students. Migrant labour from Vietnam to South Korea dates to the 1990s, and since 2004 an E-9 Employment

Permit System and C-4 seasonal visas place Vietnamese in long and short-term contract positions in factories, agriculture and aquaculture throughout the country. Marriage migration, in which South Korean men contract matchmaking agencies and arrange tours to identify suitable Vietnamese women for marriage, rose quickly in the 2000s. In 2009, 47 per cent of foreign marriages in South Korea were to Vietnamese, and the first decade of the twenty-first century alone saw the number of Vietnamese-Korean cross border marriages increase one hundred-fold (Onishi 2007; Kim 2012). Marriage migration to Korea is often associated with younger women marrying rural bachelors as well as taking on ageing in-law care duties. Driven in part by South Korea's low birth rate, ageing population, rural-urban migration, rapid industrialization, and tourism to and targeted investment in Vietnam, the demand for foreign migrants in South Korea has steadily risen. This also extends to education, where Korean universities have sought to boost declining domestic enrollment numbers by recruiting more overseas students (Nguyen 2018). Mirroring the general foreign population, Vietnamese students in South Korea rank the highest among international students, along with Chinese. There are over 44,000 Vietnamese marriage migrants, over 50,000 labourers, and over 59,000 students according to recent reports (Lee 2022; ILO 2021; Kim 2021). There is also a significant population of undocumented workers living below the official radar.

Not surprisingly these migration streams have led to various discontents and calls for intervention, including addressing the high migrant broker fees paid prior to migration and disillusionment often encountered by migrants afterwards (Song 2015). The International Organization for Migration among others has partnered with the South Korean government to provide pre-departure workshops for marriage migrants moving from Vietnam to Korea to address information and expectation asymmetries (IOM 2008). An officer running the programme in Ho Chi Minh City described the months long process as necessary to not only develop cultural adaptation skillsets and identify information resources, but also set up realistic expectations for the women who have decided to pursue immigration to Korea through marriage. On the post-arrival side, South Korea has also developed extensive general support and oversight programmes for migrant families. While primarily serving lower income households within South Korea, such programmes have been promoted as a positive development for a country generally known for its comparatively homogenous population (Lee 2014). "Multicultural Families" are celebrated as contributing to South Korea's diversity and tolerance, and programming for them provide essential support services for migrants to adapt and acculturate to Korean society.

SOUTH KOREA'S MIGRATION HISTORIES

South Korea is often stereotyped as relatively homogenous compared to other countries in the region. For example, neighbouring China officially recognizes 56 ethnic groups as part of the Chinese nation, including Korean (Asia Society). Korea, however, is a small country, additionally divided in two between North and South, and bordered by two large neighbours with long histories of imperial expansion. Resentment of the historical colonization of Korea by the Japanese empire that extended across the peninsula into neighbouring Manchuria until the mid-twentieth century, as well as Korea's long history of tributary relations to Chinese dynasties, has contributed to a contemporary national focus on identifying and celebrating cultural characteristics that are considered exclusively Korean. Such a process is always already in contest with its North Korean neighbour and complicated by the inevitable cultural flows from Korea's larger neighbours. Recent controversies have included the cultural re-appropriation by China of foods long considered uniquely Korean such as bibimbap and kimchee (Lee 2021). Trade wars between Korea and Japan over unresolved historical issues including comfort women reparations are commonplace. One unique element of Korean history and culture that has been strongly embraced has been Korea's hangul writing system. A phonetic alphabet that by now has almost completely eliminated the parallel use of some Chinese characters that were still widely taught until the late mid-twentieth century, Hangul is a strong source of national pride for Koreans. King Sejong's progressive language development campaign to extend accessible writing to the masses in the fifteenth century is widely celebrated in the Korean historiographies and the educational system, as evidenced by national holidays such as Hangul Day. As will be argued in this chapter, language also offers an avenue to incorporate new migrants into Korean society while maintaining South Korea's trend towards multicultural expansiveness.

With South Korea necessarily positioning itself as a key fulcrum to regional and global economy supply chains and capitalist growth in Asia, any lingering cultural myths of homogeneity and exclusivity are necessarily giving way to recognitions and celebrations of an emergent multicultural society. The growth of multicultural family awareness campaigns has presented South Korea with a mirror to its history and foreshadows its societal evolution. A long history of Chinese exclusion and assimilation in Korea has in many ways rendered the history of Chinese populations in the country invisible. And yet, a large ethnic Korean population in neighbouring China, including along the long Manchurian border north and west of North Korea, has led to an influx of Chinese citizens into the country. This migration pattern has been fuelled by demands for immigrant labour to support Korea's fast-growing economy. South Korea officially extends a welcoming immigration policy to ethnic Koreans anywhere in the world, from China to the former Soviet Union. In the last generation this has led in particular to a growing influx of Korean-Chinese labour migrants that have helped to economically address South Korea's labour shortage and declining birth rate. In some cases, these Chinese-Koreans include North Koreans that first crossed the border and resettled in China before attempting to then reach South Korea. The first wave of Korean international marriages in the late twentieth century often involved South Korean men and Korean-Chinese wives (Kim 2012; Lee 2022).

Given this significant and crucial labour and marriage migration stream into South Korea from China, the government of South Korea disaggregates mainland Chinese and ethnic Koreans from China in its immigration population counts. More recent migration to South Korea, however, has derived from Southeast Asia, and here the demographic trends reflect a growing regional reorientation that has been in part driven by macroeconomic policy shifts and investments.

THE NEW SOUTHERN POLICY AND SOUTHEAST ASIA

Immigration in the twentieth-first century has moved beyond the migration of Korean-Chinese to South Korea. In 2017, South Korean President Moon Jae-in launched the country's "New Southern Policy" leading to targeted foreign direct investments in Southeast Asia as part of South Korea's economic influence expansion ambitions. Korean companies have been able to mobilize significant support to invest in ASEAN markets. Hyundai, for example, went from being a relatively minor automotive player in Vietnam a decade ago to expanding its joint venture plant capacities in the country and becoming the best-selling brand in 2020 (Hyundai 2020). South Koreans are now the largest expatriate population in Vietnam, working in businesses and managing factories across the country. A number of Korean universities have also been able to secure large government grants to expand the breadth of Southeast Asian studies on their campuses, offering area studies training to Korean students and providing fellowships to Southeast Asian students to come to South Korea for their studies. Students in Vietnam say they are attracted to South Korea by their scholarship opportunities. Some are offered training opportunities by their companies that send them for degrees such as MBAs with an expectation that they will return to Vietnam with new skillsets as well as stronger cultural understandings of Korea that inevitably shape the corporate cultures they are expected to work in. Some Vietnamese students upon arriving in Korea have become aware of the struggles of their fellow nationals working as labour migrants and have organized solidarity protests to bring attention to their plights.

Indeed, a long growing trend of recruiting migrant workers from Southeast Asia has dramatically expanded. Vietnamese *phở* restaurants are now ubiquitous in Korean cities as well as small towns in rural districts, as many Southeast Asian migrants settle into Korean society and build economic livelihoods for the long term. Remittance services to facilitate monetary flows from Vietnamese resettled in South Korea take a variety of forms, from banks to courier services, and even experimentations with cryptocurrencies that can avoid the painful deductions of transfer fees. With South Korea playing a key role in ASEAN+3,[1] as well as the Regional Comprehensive Economic Partnership that is now in the process of implementation, South Korea's economic fortunes are increasingly tied with that of Southeast Asia. Within ASEAN, Korea has chosen Vietnam as a targeted country for investment, in part because of a perceived cultural and historical familiarity that goes back to wartime divisions and connections. But even those historical connections reflect an unequal and often violent relationship between the two countries (Kwon 2008).

GLOBALIZING SOUTH KOREA

As South Korea establishes itself as a major global economic player leading to population circulations in and out of the country, Korean society is becoming more multicultural. South Korean students regularly study and work abroad in countries around the world, with particularly high enrollments at U.S. post-secondary institutions. When they return home they bring new ideas, practices and relationships with them. Scholars have argued that Korea's integration and strategic placement within global markets have necessitated embodiments of capitalist subjectivities in which mobility and flexibility become valued characteristics (Kim 2020). The combination of global cosmopolitan experiences that returning Koreans bring home with them, as well as the rooted cosmopolitanism—what Benedict Anderson (2016) has suggested arrives in a society through contact with imperial and capitalist expansion and integration—that Koreans are inevitably exposed to as Korean society becomes more diverse through familiarity with labour migrants, foreign workers, spouses and long-term immigrants, has expanded not only tolerance for but also in many cases an eager acceptance of multiculturalism within the country.

In many ways this embrace of the global started with outward Korean short-term migration for work and study, but also South Korea's concerted outreach to its global diasporic population, including overseas Korean qualifications for special visas and citizenship since the 1980s (Suh 2020). More recently, however, this has institutionally expanded to a range of multicultural family and society campaigns and initiatives. These include cultural adaptation and language classes for foreigners sponsored by local government authorities, which cater to migrant labourers and migrant spouses. While in many countries foreign labour can be a contentious issue that may fuel ethnonationalism and resentment, in the case of South Korea the global flexibility that its economic and political policies promote has become in part socially and culturally embodied in its citizen outlooks and attitudes (Kim 2020). Koreans frequently travel and work abroad. Those that return, or choose to not leave as the case may be, also appear to be welcoming of the increasing multiculturalism through other migrants that are slowly remaking Korean society in the twenty-first century.

CIVIL SOCIETY SUPPORT SERVICES FOR MIGRANTS

In general, South Korea has become reflexively aware of the changing face of its societal diversity which is increasingly becoming permanent. Foreign migrants are not just cyclical but also stay as immigrants. The push for acculturation reflects a general tolerance for foreigners as long as they can linguistically and socially adapt to Korean society. Government and NGOs share the work of providing support services and disseminating information through public awareness campaigns that also build awareness among the Korean populace of the hardships that migrants face adapting to life in Korea. The Vietnamese government, through its own Ministry of Foreign Affairs and Committee for Overseas Vietnamese Affairs, also coordinates to some extent with Korea to ensure that fair policies are applied to its citizens working and living in the country.

In addition, a number of religious civil society organizations have extended social support initiatives to Vietnamese migrants. These include Buddhist organizations such as the Jongye Order, Korea's largest registered Buddhist society, that draw on the prevalence of Buddhism in Vietnam and the history and familiarity of Vietnam and Korea's shared Mahayana traditions. Social support is also provided by a range of Christian churches, both Catholic and Protestant. In some cases, support services are combined with missionary activity. In an interview with a Korean pastor and Vietnamese congregant at one Protestant church about two hours outside of Seoul, I learned that many of South Korea's over 100,000 Vietnamese live scattered throughout the country and often first arrive as agricultural labourers or as wives to Korean men in rural areas. Labour contracts are slightly under five years (four years and ten months), just short of the time required to apply for permanent residency. Marriages were also described as challenging and often leading to divorce or separation. In the case of the church there were about 40–50 multicultural Vietnamese-Korean families. Many of the Vietnamese wives in such marriages came first as labour migrants and later met their husbands or sought out matchmakers towards the ends of their agricultural labour contracts. Many of them were not Protestant prior to arriving in Korea, but found the economic and living assistance that the church provided helpful. They also went to church to support their Korean husbands and family expectations. The church in many cases provided a community organizing role to help families in need, such as women who were facing domestic abuse and isolation after divorces. Although many Vietnamese arrived on organized labour contracts that included on-site housing, over time they would learn Korean and find their way into the community to find independent accommodation and make contacts with Vietnamese in the area, often congregated at local Vietnamese restaurants or homes.

Religious organizations also offer language training, including Vietnamese for the offspring of Vietnamese-Korean marriages in order to maintain mother tongues, as well as in Korean for the purposes of acculturation and societal and employment survival. Language classes offered by religious organizations are typically shorter in format, offered for example on Sundays after services. The linguistic training they provide while helpful and convenient, especially for a busy migrant worker population, is of course not as substantive as daily classes provided by the government through multicultural family centres.

GOVERNMENT MULTICULTURAL TRAINING AND SPACE MAKING

In the Summer of 2019 and Fall of 2020 I participated in two Seoul district level government run migrant classes for multicultural families designed to support and teach Korean language to foreign spouses living in the country. One was in person, and the other, due to the onset of the COVID-19 pandemic in 2020, was online. The latter turned out to be an accidental opportunity for reoriented participant observation, what Marilyn Strathern might call an "ethnographic moment". I was on sabbatical leave, intending to head to Vietnam for field research. I had stopped en-route in Seoul with my family in August of 2020 to visit my Korean in-laws. However, due to the border closures in Vietnam and indeed across the region at that time, my family ended up staying in Korea until December. Since I was officially a migrant spouse, being married to a South Korean citizen, I found myself eligible for the full length of a fall language course and enrolled. Other students in the course hailed from China, Vietnam, Myanmar, and Cambodia, with one Venezuelan, one British and one American (myself) also in the mix. Over 80 per cent of the participants were female, and after Chinese, Vietnamese represented the largest national group, hailing from both northern and southern

Vietnam. Over the course of four months of participation I found the classes to be professional and rigourous, and conducive to building community among the students via the "lingua franca" of Korean across migrants of different national origins. The course was entirely free except for the cost of books. The classes I participated in were four times a week on weekdays. A foundation in Hangul reading and writing was strongly emphasized in the pedagogy.

A separate Foreign Worker Center course offering that I did not follow concentrated teaching in longer blocs on Sundays. The weekend course was designed for migrant labourers who were likely working Monday through Saturday and would not have time to join the weekday spouse class. During class sessions the instructor covered approximately one learning unit every two days, split between two books specializing in grammatical patterns and reading and listening comprehension. Topics were typical for first year language curriculums—shopping, activities, family etc., although there was a clear multicultural dimension in which many featured characters in the dialogues originated from countries in the region such as the Philippines.

What was particularly interesting about the pedagogical design for the target learning community were the attached extracurricular options. Although the classes I attended in 2020 were mostly held online, during periods of flattening COVID-19 infections the government would allow for more public openings and gatherings. During such times the multicultural family support centre would occasionally offer get togethers that ranged from cooking classes to outings to cultural sites in the city of Seoul and beyond. These activities had been commonplace in my previous albeit shorter experience with a Korean multicultural centre language class in 2019. Students were also introduced to specialized television programmes for migrant workers, as well as practical life skill/needs orientations such as driving and shopping sessions. Overall, however, the availability of online classes expanded the ability of many migrant spouses to attend classes, as the virtual format reduced time lost in commuting and lost income from labouring in other occupations.

South Korean municipalities host multicultural family websites providing a range of information and services for foreign migrants. Activities include meetings to discuss challenges of navigating the pandemic, social integration seminars, family counselling, public health advisories, health insurance workshops, migrant children childcare and education, domestic abuse shelters, medical interpretation, leisure sports gatherings, college admission workshops, and job fairs among others. Foreign language radio stations such as TBS in Seoul featuring DJs that are themselves diasporic Korean and bilingual, share information about living support programmes in South Korea, for example the Oneness Festival that invites foreigner nationals, naturalized citizens, and Koreans with a foreign parent to submit K-Pop cover song singing videos for competition. The Oneness competition videos do not include the face of the competitor, emphasizing therefore the "oneness" or ability of migrants to acculturate through language in which judges cannot differentiate the linguistic ability of a foreigner versus a native Korean. Such services as well as celebrations are certainly helpful for migrants, and in line with many of the policy recommendations compiled by international organizations and NGOs dealing with Vietnamese migration to Korea over the years on enhancing transparent information access and social support capacities (Park 2017).

LANGUAGE AND COMMUNITY

At the end of the beginner Korean course in December 2020, the teacher and coordinator offered an online satisfaction survey translated into all the languages of the class participants—from Khmer to Chinese to Vietnamese. Many of the students giggled when they saw the questions in their own native languages, inevitably replete with grammatical and spelling errors. Afterwards, an orphaned group of Kakao[2] social media profiles served as a reminder of the unique language learning community that had diligently come together an hour and a half a day, four days a week, for four months. Despite being occasionally pulled away for family duties such as kimchi preparation, child care and family travels, the students' command of Korean had grown exponentially during the course (and far outpacing what I could keep up with). Building a solid foundation of Korean language, combined with the South Korean society adaptation workshops, were surely helpful for (im)migrants navigating their way in a new linguistic and cultural landscape that was distant, isolated and cold compared to Vietnam and most of the other participants' Southeast Asian origin countries. For many who felt stuck in Korea during the pandemic due to the closure of borders, such daily gatherings also served as a source of comfort and shared forum of frustration at the immobility experienced by many Asian migrants between 2020 and 2022. As one of the Vietnamese students lamented to the rest of us, "I miss my family, my culture, and my food so much."

But another outcome was that the class had cultivated a sense of community among the students, connecting them beyond the individual households many of them married into. In that class space and its virtual aftermath, Korean language became a common medium of exchange, offering migrants a space to share and reminisce on their own trajectories that brought them to South Korea as well as the unique cultural contributions each of them offered in their new environments. While the larger groups of Vietnamese and Chinese speakers in particular tended to speak with each other in their native languages at the start of the course, by the end, students across all nationality groups from Burmese to Khmer were making connections using basic Korean. A week after the class ended, on the first of January 2021 the Kakao group messaging function lit up with a flurry of "새해 복 많이 받으세요" (Happy New Year) exchanges as students reconnected to well wish each other for the start of 2022.

Benedict Anderson, reflecting on the structural inequalities of international migration, observed that "the segregated queues that all of us experience at airport immigration barricades mark economic status far more than any political attachments. In effect, they figure differential tariffs on human labour" (Anderson 1998). This is certainly the case of labour and marriage migration to South Korea, and demonstrative that the country's continued economic progression relies on a socioeconomically tiered transnational economy of regionally imported intimate and physical labour. Yet it is Anderson's analysis of the affective communities facilitated by shared language groups that is most well-known. Anderson connects language to the birth of nationalism, arguing that the expansion of print media facilitated an awareness of shared language communities and by extension national groups. As people began to read vernacular newspapers they started to build emotive shared connections with others sharing the same language community in distant places that in the past would have felt disconnected. Shared language connections were the basis for what he called "imagined communities" (Anderson 1991). Anderson also argued that the experience of removal from one's homeland helped build this sense of imagined community, coined as "long distance nationalism".

Language has always been an important site of analysis for Anderson, as he argued that language serves as more than just a tool for communication. "To learn a language ... is also to learn the way of thinking and feeling of a people who speak and write a language which is different ... It is to learn the history and culture underlying their thoughts and emotions and so to learn to empathize with them" (Anderson 2016, p. 70). In the case of migrants in South Korea, one can see how the intention of multicultural family centres with their strong focus on language acquisition starting with Hangul is entangled with this goal to help immigrants understand the history, culture, thoughts and emotions of their country of resettlement. But the effect of learning the Korean language also serves to cultivate a community of speakers who are building ties to more than just the national body politic of South Korea. Their removal from home furthermore does not just fuel a long-distance sense of diasporic nationalism. Rather, the shared process of learning Korean as foreigners from different countries helps to build communicative avenues with other migrants. Through Korean language learning, Cambodians, Chinese, Vietnamese, Burmese and others in such classes are able to develop a medium through which to share experiences and stories with each other as they collectively go through a parallel process of adapting to life in a foreign land. As much as multiculturalism is emergent and on the rise for South Koreans, it is equally central to the lives of migrants for whom finding a place of their own in the country means not just culturally adapting to Korea, but also learning about and connecting to other migrants that can empathize with their migration pathways and acculturation expectations. Language, long distance nationalism, and community building all come together in these entangled processes of multicultural migration connections and language acquisition, but in a somewhat different formulation than Anderson dyadically analysed. Indeed, Korean language acquisition in the context of migrant classes produced a consciousness of shared migrant-ness in Korea, heightened during the immobility of the pandemic, in which connections with others fostered a community that was neither homeland gazing nor host country assimilating.

CONCLUSION

South Korea is acutely aware of its growing multiculturalism. There is especially a growing orientation to Southeast Asia in line with Korean regional investment patterns and free trade agreements. Popular television shows depict Koreans exploring new culinary and cultural adventures across a number of ASEAN countries. In Vietnamese universities, Koreans represent some of the highest foreign student enrollments for Vietnamese language classes, and Korean expatriates are ubiquitous in cities like Hanoi and Ho Chi Minh, comprising the largest foreign population in Vietnam. Korean media also regularly reports on migrants in South Korea, ranging from the labours that they contribute to the country's economy—unloading fish catches for example in the busy port of Incheon and planting and harvesting rice in South Korea's under-staffed rural districts. Vietnam's soccer team coached by a Korean is popularly followed in South Korea. Korean media has also been reporting on cases of the increasingly well documented domestic abuses of Vietnamese women by Korean husbands, contributing to outrage among many Koreans. Yet the growing awareness of Vietnamese migrants also at times lends to suspicions of their motives. On more than one occasion I heard rumours in Korea by Koreans about Vietnamese women who were already married in Vietnam that nonetheless dishonestly came to Korea to marry Korean men, bore children who have full citizenship rights, and then proceeded to divorce the Korean husband and bring the original husband over through legal immigration channels due to the child's citizenship status. In one rural district that I visited there was a story about a Korean man who died of sadness in the aftermath of his Vietnamese wife leaving him. The house that they once lived in together still sits empty after many years.

Nonetheless, there is a commonly expressed sentiment that through language acquisition, foreigners, and especially Asians that look more similar to Koreans such as Vietnamese, can acculturate to Korean society. This is not always seen to be the case with migrants from other ethnic groups, as a recent controversy over Yemeni refugees on Jeju island illustrates (Kwon 2019). The growth of South Korea's multicultural family support programmes including language training is undoubtedly a valuable resource for the country's growing migrant and now immigrant population. Whether such classes and other multicultural campaigns can or should assimilate migrants to "Korea" is debatable. Assimilation presumes a one-way street of acculturation to host societies and a dilution of migrant cultural traditions. Discussions about who is assimilable and who is not will likely simmer as the scope of migrant and refugee acceptance expands. But more significantly I would argue, language programmes are valuable precisely because they have expanded the parameters of what it means to be Korean in the twenty-first century. This includes foreign spouses, workers, students and other immigrants, and is partly gauged on the acquisition of language, which is feasible even if the next level of cultural adaptation that proponents envision may not be so easily achievable or desirable. Most importantly however, language classes have helped foster a space for connections among migrants from diverse cultural and linguistic backgrounds that are all trying to make their way in Korean society. Such connections and potential solidarities among them will certainly be one of the longer-term results of South Korea's migrant adaptation and multicultural programming, whether intentional in design or not.

NOTES

1. Association of Southeast Asian Nations plus China, South Korea and Japan.
2. Kakao is a social communication application, similar to Whatsapp, particularly popular in South Korea.

REFERENCES

Anderson, Benedict. 1991. *Imagined Communities*. London: Verso.
_____. 1998. *The Spectre of Comparisons*. London: Verso.
_____. 2016. *A Life Beyond Boundaries*. London: Verso.
BBC News. 2019. "South Korea and Japan's Feud Explained", 2 December 2019. https://www.bbc.com/news/world-asia-49330531.
Consular Department, Ministry of Foreign Affairs of Viet Nam. 2012. *Review of Vietnamese Migration Abroad*. https://eeas.europa.eu/archives/delegations/vietnam/documents/eu_vietnam/vn_migration_abroad_en.pdf.
Dede, Keith. N.d. "Ethnic Minorities in China: The Mongols, Tibetans, Manchus, and Naxi". Asia Society. https://asiasociety.org/ethnic-minorities-china.

Employment Permit System, Republic of Korea. N.d. https://www.eps.go.kr.
Hyundai Motor Co. 2020. "Hyundai Dominates the Vietnamese Market", 7 July 2020. https://www.hyundaimotorgroup.com/story/CONT0000000000003257.
International Labour Organization (ILO). 2021. "TRIANGLE in ASEAN Quarterly Briefing Note", Viet Nam January–June 2022. https://www.ilo.org/wcmsp5/groups/public/---asia/---ro-bangkok/documents/genericdocument/wcms_735109.pdf.
International Organization for Migration (IOM). 2008. "Migrant Rights". *Migration* (July). https://www.iom.int/sites/default/files/our_work/ICP/IDM/Migration_July08_EN.pdf.
Kim, Hee-Kang. 2012. "Marriage Migration Between South Korea and Vietnam". *Asian Perspective* 36, no. 3.
Kim, Na-Rae. 2020. "Global South Korea in 21st Century Asian American Literature". In *Oxford Encyclopedia of Asian American Literature and Culture*, edited by Josephine Lee. Oxford: Oxford University Press.
Kim, Yon-se. 2021. "7 in 10 Foreign Students are Vietnamese or Chinese". *Korea Herald*, 29 April 2021. http://www.koreaherald.com/view.php?ud=20210429000268.
Kwon, Heonik. 2008. *Ghosts of War in Vietnam*. Cambridge: Cambridge University Press.
Kwon, Jeeyun. 2019. "South Korea's Yemeni Refugee Problem". MEI, 23 April 2019. https://www.mei.edu/publications/south-koreas-yemeni-refugee-problem.
Lee, Gyu-lee. 2021. "Chinese Bibimbap in Vincenzo Stirs Up Korean Viewers". *Korea Times*, 15 March 2021). https://www.koreatimes.co.kr/www/art/2021/03/688_305562.html.
Lee, Hyunok. 2014. "Trafficking in Women? Or Multicultural Family?" *Gender, Place & Culture* 21, no. 10: 1249–66.
———. 2022. "Global Householding and Gendered Citizenship". *Asian and Pacific Migration Journal* 31, no. 1.
Multicultural Family website, South Korea. N.d. https://www.mcfamily.or.kr/intro_web.php.
Nguyen, Quy. 2018. "Number of Vietnamese Students in South Korea Grow Fastest in World". *VN Express*, 16 October 2018. https://e.vnexpress.net/news/news/number-of-vietnamese-students-in-south-korea-grow-fastest-in-the-world-3824515.html.
Onishi, Norimitsu. 2007. "Marriage Brokers in Vietnam Cater to South Korean Bachelors". *New York Times*, 21 February 2007. https://www.nytimes.com/2007/02/21/world/asia/21iht-brides.4670360.html.
Park, Si-Soo. 2018. "Foreign Population Jumps to 2.18 Million". *Korea Times*, 25 January 2018. https://www.koreatimes.co.kr/www/nation/2018/01/177_243054.html.

Park, Young-bum. 2017. "South Korea Carefully Tests the Waters on Immigration, with a Focus on Temporary Workers". Migration Policy Institute, 1 March 2017. https://www.migrationpolicy.org/article/south-korea-carefully-tests-waters-immigration-focus-temporary-workers.

Song, Jiyoung. 2015. "Five Phases of Brokered International Marriages in South Korea: A Complexity Perspective". *Asian Studies* 1, no. 1: 147–76.

Strathern, Marilyn. 2022. *Property, Substance and Effect.* Chicago: University of Chicago Press.

Suh, Stephen Cho. 2020. "Nostalgia for the Unfamiliar: Korean Americans' 'Imagined Affective Connection' to the Ancestral Homeland". *Ethnicities* 22, no. 1.

6

"FOREIGN TALENT" IN SINGAPORE AND SOME IMPLICATIONS FOR SCHOOLS

Jason Tan and Lana Khong

INTRODUCTION

Singapore's population policy in the last three decades, given sub-replacement fertility rates, has been to directly inject new blood into the local community. Skilled foreign professionals have been drawn mainly from so-called "indigenous sources", namely China and India, undergirded by the assumption that an infusion of people from these two countries would be relatively painless for social and cultural assimilation since Singapore has an incumbent ethnic Chinese and Indian population. However, there is plenty of evidence that the process could be bumpier than policymakers expected. Schools, to a large extent directly mirroring national undercurrents, offer a window through which to examine the competitive dynamics emerging from a "replacement migration" of ethnically-similar but culturally-distinct people groups. The chapter examines critical aspects of education policy such as the admission of foreign-born students, the awarding of scholarships to foreign-born students and the recruitment of foreign-born teachers.

Our chapter is framed by a wider narrative on the government's long-standing policy of drawing in, in large numbers over the years, what it has termed "foreign talent"[1] to augment the local workforce. For instance, it was reported in 2020 that Singaporeans made up about 43 per cent of senior management across the entire financial sector (Lam and Ng 2020). The official approach in justifying this move has been to help "grow the economic pie" for Singapore which is then expected to expand to benefit locals as well.

However, the onslaught of the COVID-19 pandemic in 2020 has brought about an official re-assessment of immigration policy. In a live televised debate during the July 2020 election campaign period, the Foreign Minister went so far as to state that

> [t]he only reason we have foreigners here is to give an extra wind in our sails when the opportunity is there ... Now we are in a storm and we need to shed ballast ... 60,000 foreigners have lost their jobs. And the schemes we have rolled out now ... (are) clearly slanted at Singaporeans.

In the immediate aftermath of the elections, which saw the ruling People's Action Party losing two Group Representation Constituencies, the Manpower Ministry started to "shed ballast" by announcing that the minimum salary requirements for foreign PMETs working here will be raised. Thus, foreigners who apply for an Employment Pass (EP) will need to have a minimum monthly salary of $4,500, up from $3,900. From December 2020, EP holders in the financial sector will need a minimum salary of $5,000 (Ministry of Manpower 2021a). For mid-skilled foreigners on the Short-term Employment Pass (S Pass), the qualifying salary has also been raised from $2,400 to $2,500 (Ministry of Manpower 2021b). The explicit purpose of these recent manpower policy changes is to push employers to hire more locals in the "storm" of growing job insecurity and economic recession triggered by the pandemic. In a similar vein, Indranee Rajah, the Minister in the Prime Minister's Office and Second Minister for National Development, told Parliament in February 2021 about the need to balance "a workforce with a strong Singaporean core" with "an economy that is open to global skills":

> We must also remain open to global talent who can complement our local workforce, and attract high-value activities that create quality jobs for locals. This is why we have tightened the EP criteria. ... We set a high bar ... and are very selective. The talent base will help us emerge stronger, by anchoring and expanding new growth sectors ... we will continue to carefully calibrate the pace of immigration. (Rajah 2021)

A serious consequence linked to the overall political and economic agenda for welcoming a large influx of foreigners into Singapore over the past three decades without a deliberate policy to also gradually integrate them into local communities is a growing local-foreigner divide and rising anti-foreigner sentiments on the ground. These are triggered by a local perception of increasing diversity and competition within limited common spaces such as public housing, transportation, work and schools (see for instance, Mathews et al. 2019; Mathews and Zhang 2016). The Population White Paper published in 2013 reinforced the public's perception that immigration remains a long-term go-to approach of the government with the total population target set between 6.5 million and 6.9 million by 2030. Of the resident population projected by then to be 4.2 million to 4.4 million, citizens make up just 3.6 million to 3.8 million (approximately 55 per cent). Between 2000 and 2015, the number of non-residents who live and work in Singapore increased from 0.75 million to 1.63 million. At the same time, the resident fertility rate hovered at 1.12 in 2021, clearly inadequate for meeting Singapore's economic requirements. These developments have engendered widespread citizen criticism and fuelled increasing anti-foreigner sentiments in both offline and online spaces. It continues to be a hot issue that threatens the fragile fabric of social cohesion in the nation and, going forward in a COVID-19 world, needs careful, deliberate and sensitive management on several fronts by policymakers to prevent it tearing further. For instance, the managing director of the Monetary Authority of Singapore recently called for the tightening of salary criteria for foreign workers and the stemming of discriminatory hiring practices in order to ensure what he termed "a strong Singaporean core" of workers to "work alongside the best global talents" (Ho 2021b). The public furore over foreigners in the workforce is occurring alongside renewed discussions about racism in the public sphere and in schools (see for instance, Davie and Ng 2021; Lim 2021; Wong 2021).

This chapter will share our observations of some challenging dynamics operating in the competitive national school domain as a directly related issue. These are the roles of schools in promoting a common national identity, as well as Ministry of Education decisions with regard to school admission policies, the provision of government-funded scholarships for international students, the recruitment of foreign-born teachers and efforts to promote integration of foreign-born students within schools. The central message is that the task of managing education policy amid the political and social tensions brought about by immigration policy remains arduous.

IMPLICATIONS FOR SCHOOLS

Diversity or Divisiveness?

The Singapore school system, as in other culturally-diverse nations elsewhere, is enlisted to not only provide successive student cohorts with competitive, marketable skills to help them eventually contribute to the economic survival of the nation but also, to perform an essential nation-building function, that is, to strengthen social cohesion and effectively weave together its multi-ethnic, multi-cultural student bodies, including foreign-born students (and teachers). Different school structures, curricula and initiatives such as the Co-Curricular Activities (CCA), Character and Citizenship Education (CCE) and Values in Action (VIA) programmes are compulsory for all students throughout primary, secondary, and tertiary levels of mainstream schooling, establishing shared common spaces for the young to mingle, work together, and build friendships. The task of social integration in schools has been made more complex with the growing emergence of cross-national marriages (Tan 2021) and the widening of social inequalities (Teng 2019). The local vs foreigner debate has undoubtedly thrown additional fuel on to these fires of contention. For instance, the debate over allowing foreign professionals to work in Singapore (Ho 2021a) has coincided with calls for fresh approaches to the promotion of multicultural education in schools (Davie 2021) and public concern over racism in schools (Yeoh 2021; Zakaria 2021).

The official rhetoric in schools and institutes of higher education, seen as natural bridge-building platforms and a key "touchpoint" for integration, is an inclusive one and is bolstered by one of four working groups in the National Integration Council (NIC) set up in 2009. The NIC-Schools working group explicates three "tiers of integration", namely functional integration, developing social networks, and promoting mutual trust and understanding, voicing tolerance, even appreciation, for cultural diversity. Schools and educational institutions have been encouraged by the Ministry of Education to implement various schemes such as "peer support ambassadors" or "homestay programmes" in order to help foreign students adjust to school life.

Despite these laudable measures, it is common to see and hear anecdotal evidence of unflattering generalizations and negative stereotypes expressed reciprocally between local and foreign school stakeholders such as students, parents or even teachers, regarding different cultural attitudes, backgrounds, habits, and practices. Integration, as the other side of the coin of immigration, is thus still a work in progress and schools, as mirrors of the wider community, offer a window through which to examine the competitive dynamics emerging from a "replacement migration" of ethnically-similar but culturally-distinct people, especially the foreign Chinese and Indian group.

School Admission Policies

Over the past few decades, Singapore's school system has been characterized as being highly competitive. Under the national ideology of meritocracy, students' performance in a series of key high-stakes national examinations at both primary and secondary levels has been a major determinant in their educational success and socio-economic mobility (Tan 2010). Despite official efforts by the Ministry of Education to reduce the competitive stress faced by schoolchildren, there is ample evidence that many parents still view schooling as an educational "arms race" and are still not entirely convinced of the mantra "Every school is a good school." The Prime Minister, in his 2013 National Day rally, commented that there still remains intense competition to gain admission to popular primary schools (Dorai 2017).

The primary school admission system has in the last few years been amended to give clear priority to the children of Singaporean citizens over those of permanent residents and those of parents who are neither citizens nor permanent residents. These changes have been made on top of the long-standing practice of giving priority to the children of Singaporeans and permanent residents. In 2016, the Education Ministry claimed that "the proportions of international students and PR [permanent resident] students in local schools have remained fairly constant in recent years, at 4 and 9 percent respectively." The same article highlighted the increasing difficulty that expatriate parents, including those who were permanent residents, were experiencing in enrolling their children in local schools. A Ministry spokesman said that while it valued the diversity that foreign students could bring to the school system, it had to prioritize the needs of Singaporeans (Teng 2016a). A more recent Ministry estimate was that international students made up about 5 per cent of all students in primary and secondary schools and junior colleges (Chia and Smalley 2021).

Beginning in 2018, the Ministry revised its annual primary one registration exercise to introduce an additional step in the application process for international students who were not the children of citizens or permanent residents. Its press statement acknowledged the fact that a growing number of such students had been applying for admission to local primary schools (Ministry of Education 2018). In 2020, the registration exercise was changed yet again with the introduction of a cap of about 25 to 30 per cent on the children of permanent residents in ten primary schools. The official rationale was the prevention of any concentration of such children in primary schools in order to facilitate more interaction between them and Singapore citizens, and also to promote the integration of the children of permanent residents into Singapore (Ministry of Education 2020a).

Further measures to restrict the entry of non-citizens into local schools include progressive increases in school fees for non-citizens in order to "further differentiate fees by citizenship". The latest round of fee increases began in 2016 and lasted into 2020, with further increases announced in 2021 for 2022 and 2023 (see Tables 6.1, 6.2 and 6.3). Of particular note is the fact that the fees for citizens have remained constant amid these fee increases for non-citizens. The combination of reduced admission chances into local schools and repeated fee increases has driven some expatriate families to try the more expensive international schools (Teng 2016b). However, the exact scale of the

TABLE 6.1
Primary School Fees (Singapore dollars, monthly)

Nationality	2015	2016	2017	2018	2019	2020	2022	2023
Citizen	Free							
Permanent Resident	90	110	130	155	180	205	230	255
International Student (ASEAN)	350	370	390	415	440	465	490	515
International Student	500	550	600	650	700	750	825	875

Sources: Ministry of Education (2015, 2016, 2017, 2021).

TABLE 6.2
Secondary School Fees (Singapore dollars, monthly)

Nationality	2015	2016	2017	2018	2019	2020	2022	2023
Citizen	5	5	5	5	5	5	5	5
Permanent Resident	120	160	200	260	320	380	440	500
International Student (ASEAN)	450	550	600	660	720	780	840	900
International Student	650	800	950	1,100	1,250	1,400	1,600	1,750

Sources: Ministry of Education (2015, 2016, 2017, 2021).

TABLE 6.3
Pre-university School Fees (Singapore dollars, monthly)

Nationality	2015	2016	2017	2018	2019	2020	2022	2023
Citizen	6	6	6	6	6	6	6	6
Permanent Resident	160	220	280	340	400	460	520	580
International Student (ASEAN)	700	800	860	920	980	1,040	1,070	1,100
International Student	1,000	1,150	1,300	1,450	1,600	1,750	1,950	2,100

Sources: Ministry of Education (2015, 2016, 2017, 2021).

impact of these difficulties on expatriates' plans to relocate away from Singapore, as well as the plans of prospective expatriates to Singapore, is still unknown.

Scholarships for International Students

The tensions over foreign students in local schools have also extended to the enrolment of these students in local universities as well as the granting of generous scholarships to some of these students. Singapore has had a long-standing policy of encouraging foreign student enrolment in local universities. In the 1980s it announced a 20 per cent target for such enrolments. In reaction to concerns raised by Singaporeans about the concomitant detrimental effects on the enrolment of local students, the government has stated that Singaporean students will be granted first priority for admission. In addition, foreign students have to meet more stringent admission requirements than local students (see for instance, Parliamentary Debates, 45, 1985, Cols. 1444–1446; 58, 1991, Cols. 46, 63).

Its rationale for admitting international students is four-fold. First, all foreign students who receive Singapore government subsidies in the form of tuition fee grants have to sign a bond to live and work in Singapore for at least three years upon graduation, thus adding to the local talent pool. Admitting them is thus a prime investment as local taxpayers have not had to pay for their prior education. Secondly, Singapore needs to compete aggressively in the burgeoning world education market. Thirdly, local students will benefit from interacting with foreign students and learning about different cultures, thus placing them in a more competitive position within the global economy. Furthermore, the government hopes that when these foreign students return to their home countries, they will form a global network that is favourably predisposed towards Singapore (see for instance, Parliamentary Debates, 45, 1985, Col. 1447; 50, 1988, Cols. 1103–1104; 58, 1991, Cols. 63–64).

In a 2020 parliamentary reply, the Ministry of Education revealed that less than 10 per cent of each local publicly-funded university intake consists of international students who receive undergraduate scholarships and tuition grants. It stated that figures over the past three years indicated that the relative percentages of international students on tuition grant only, those on a combination of tuition grant and scholarships, and those who are full-fee paying (i.e., not in receipt of either a tuition grant or a scholarship) were "about" 60, 25 and 15 respectively (Ministry of Education 2020b). The reply also disclosed that about 75 per cent of scholarship holders and 60 per cent of tuition grant recipients from the 2012 to 2014 graduation cohorts had been granted permanent residence, with about 10 to 15 per cent eventually becoming citizens within five years of graduation. The Ministry reiterated its long-standing hope that foreign students who left Singapore after graduation would "continue to be part of our valuable global network, through the friendships and links forged during their studies".

The COVID-19 pandemic has had a direct effect on admissions policies in the six local autonomous universities. The Ministry of Education has allowed each of these universities to increase their enrolments of Singapore citizens in order to address the issue of students' overseas study plans being disrupted. Consequently, the autonomous universities have admitted an additional 1,000 Singapore students in the 2020 and 2021 academic years (Ang 2021). At the same time, the pandemic has probably led to a decline in international student enrolments in the autonomous universities over 2020 and 2021, although exact figures are unavailable (Teng 2022).

Recruiting Foreign-born Teachers

Hardly anything is known about foreign-born teachers who have not been students themselves in Singapore schools, but who arrived in Singapore either during or after their undergraduate years. Yang and Chow (2019) cite a 2011 news article that estimated these teachers form 2 per cent of the total number of teachers in local mainstream schools. The vast majority of the respondents in Yang and Chow's research study were from The People's Republic of China and Malaysia, and were teaching Chinese Language, a figure which suggests a shortage of suitably qualified locals. Overall, about 80 per cent of foreign-born teachers are recruited as Mother Tongue Language teachers. Some of the major issues that these immigrant teachers grapple with, as Yang and Chow term them, included a lack of fluency in English, the dominant language in Singapore schools. They felt that this language barrier disadvantaged these teachers in circumstances when they had to teach in English, for example, during Character and Citizenship Education lessons in secondary schools. Teachers themselves reported that this lack of fluency in English also hindered their social and professional integration. Next, while they felt that their individual life experiences outside of Singapore might have the potential to enrich the lessons, they also thought that their inevitable lack of local experiences and more superficial cultural knowledge might hinder their ability to build rapport with local students. Furthermore, Yang and Chow found that some of these teachers' personal beliefs, values and practices could at times to be at odds with the dominant narratives in Singapore schools, for instance, with regard to sexuality education and character and citizenship education. Yet at the same time, they were also required to carry themselves as "agents" of the Ministry of Education and pillars of the education system as a whole, regardless of their subject specializations.

A decade later, the Ministry of Education provided statistics that indicated the number of foreign-born teachers had nearly halved since 2011, and that these teachers now form less than 1 per cent of the overall teaching force. The Ministry claimed that this drop was in tandem with falling student enrolments (from 510,714 in 2010 to 424,402 in 2019) and was also an indication of an adequate supply of local teachers. These teachers were mainly from China, Malaysia, Indonesia, France and Spain, and had been recruited to teach subjects such as mother tongue and third languages (Ong 2021b). The Education Ministry also acknowledged that foreign-born teachers could play a vital role in "broadening students' horizons, understanding cultural differences and leveraging opportunities within and beyond Singapore" (Ong 2021a). To date, there has been no research on the ways in which foreign-born teachers play this role, or the effect of the reduction in the number of foreign-born teachers on students' inter-cultural awareness.

Intentional Integration

Before the NIC was set up, policymakers had made the rather *laissez-faire* assumption that "new residents" mostly drawn from China and the Indian subcontinent, would assimilate naturally since they already shared similar ethnic identities with locals. There has emerged in recent years therefore an *intra-ethnic* local-foreign divide that is complicated by the fact that most recent Indian immigrants (many high-flyers in the PMET sectors) are North Indian and of the Brahmin caste, whereas local second- and third-generation Indian families originally hailed from South India and are less active adherents to the traditional Indian caste system. This has led to tensions between Indian immigrants and local Indians regarding language, culture and even, religious rituals. The growing number of new immigrants and Indians on EPs has led to demands for Hindi to be taught in local schools. These demands are viewed by Singapore Indians are a threat to the traditional dominance of Singaporean Tamils. Locally-born Indians are also being criticized by recent Indian immigrants for their "inauthentic" adaptations of religious temple practices, as well as "contamination" in the areas of food, dance and music (see for instance, Kathiravelu 2020).

Similar tensions simmer between locals and their counterparts from China (see for instance, Ho and Foo 2020). It is estimated that there are between 13,000 and 15,000 Mainland Chinese students studying in Singapore, accounting for at least one-third of international students here. When Mainland Chinese adults are spotlighted for behaviours such as insisting on speaking Mandarin to non-Chinese locals, spitting, not queuing in an orderly manner, littering, cheating landlords of rental fees, or even defecating in public places, these are immediately roundly decried by some locals as barbaric, uncouth and decidedly un-Singaporean. If and when these occur in the school setting, some children or even teachers may resort to ridicule, bullying and exclusion of these foreign-born students. Sometimes, it is the foreign students themselves who are the cause of strong backlash. For instance, in 2012 a student from Mainland China caused public outrage with his derogatory online comments about Singaporeans (Chen 2012).

Now that the gates have been opened, the rising tide of global immigration and increased multi-culturalism in Singapore cannot easily be stemmed and, while we are not at the stage of complete integration of all groups in the Singapore collective (even if that were possible), greater awareness of and sensitivity to the challenges means that progress can continue to be made, albeit slowly. It is encouraging to see that positive changes are happening on the ground and from the ground-up, starting with our younger generation, but while that is necessary, it may not be sufficient to set off a continuous positive ripple into society at large.

CONCLUSION

How Now, the "Singaporean Core"?

This chapter has presented the implications of immigration for education policy in Singapore. The Education Ministry has had to react to the sentiments of some local-born Singaporeans over the enrolment of non-Singaporean students in schools and the provision of government-funded scholarships for foreign-born students. It has also implemented measures to promote integration in schools and halved the number of foreign-born teachers in national schools.

When large-scale immigration is used as the solution to buffer national manpower shortfalls amid declining fertility rates, social diversity is inevitable and "enclave societies" may be formed if there are sufficiently large numbers of such economic migrants. They will tend to coalesce together, form their own clubs and societies or live in the same neighbourhoods (see for instance, Elangovan 2021a), to reinforce familiar cultural comfort zones and as a result, may appear unfriendly or even hostile to locals. Authentic assimilation or integration is then hindered, leading to an escalation of further more negative perceptions of the newcomers, especially when they are also seen as unwelcome competitors in the workplace or school settings. Integration, according to experts, and "becoming Singaporean" is a reciprocal process that takes place over a long time: foreigners must want to integrate and commit themselves to contributing to Singapore, and locals must be open enough to accept and make them feel they belong here. It will take nothing short of a national mindset change to make it happen, as well as requiring a persistent and consistent whole-of-government effort to intentionally develop an innate "intercultural intelligence" in the next generation of adults. The absence of more thoughtful and calibrated approaches to immigration and integration, particularly during times of intense economic uncertainty and growing societal inequalities, has the potential to exacerbate divisiveness and mutual antagonism (Lai 2012). The economic and social disruptions caused by the COVID-19 pandemic are probably linked with the upsurge in public discussion about racism (Ong 2021c) and the role that schools play in countering it (Elangovan 2021b).

If the "Singaporean core" is about the intangibles of spirit and values, as the Prime Minister has said, much remains to be done to seed plant and grow these instinctive qualities in our young. In schools, teachers play an especially important part in the slow but powerful process of changing attitudes and mindsets of the younger generation but they will need new mindsets as well as skillsets themselves for observing, empathizing, and mediating ethno-cultural tensions in classrooms and school spaces before these can escalate. For example, they must make it clear to their students that there is zero tolerance for racist comments or demeaning jokes that put down others just because they look different, or do things, or speak differently. This should apply equally to both local-born and foreign-born students. Teachers' expectations and treatment of students must first set the tone for a cohesive classroom and school community, one that highlights equity, impartiality, care and concern for all students, regardless of their ethnicity or nationality. We expect that teachers will have to play an increasingly important role as cultural brokers in this important evolution of our society. The question is "How can they, as products of their own upbringing, most effectively perform this critical role and how must we, as the rest of the community, most fruitfully imagine, manage and support them in meeting contribution to this strenuous challenge?" Teachers will need to examine their own biases and prejudices (Davie and Ng 2021), as well as those in the wider community, while possessing the moral courage to confront them in an honest manner with their students, in order for progress to be made in the task of addressing the social fissures that have emerged as a result of large-scale immigration into Singapore.

NOTE

1. The term 'foreign talent' in Singapore commonly refers to skilled workers such as professionals, managers, executives and technicians.

REFERENCES

Ang, Hwee Min. 2021. "About 1,000 More Students Admitted into Singapore's Autonomous Universities in AY2021: MOE". *Channel NewsAsia Online*, 29 October 2021. https://www.channelnewsasia.com/singapore/covid-19-1000-more-students-admitted-universities-ay2021-moe-2277101 (accessed 11 April 2022).

Chen, Clarence. 2012. "S'poreans Outraged Over PRC Scholar's 'Dog' Comment". *Yahoo! News Singapore*, 22 February 2012. https://sg.news.yahoo.com/blogs/singaporescene/poreans-outraged-over-prc-scholar-dog-072146916.html (accessed 23 March 2021).

Chia, Lianne and Ruth Smalley. 2021. "Friends From Other Lands: The Unique Challenges of International Students at One Primary School". *Channel NewsAsia Online*, 3 February 2021. https://www.channelnewsasia.com/news/cnainsider/international-students-singapore-primary-school-farrer-park-12139974 (accessed 25 July 2021).

Davie, Sandra. 2021. "Time to Shift From 'Tourist Approach' in Teaching About Other Cultures". *The Straits Times*, 21 July 2021, p. A16.

Davie, Sandra and Ng Wei Kai. 2021. "Tackling Issues About Race in Classrooms". *The Straits Times*, 25 June 2021, pp. B1, B2.

Dorai, Francis. 2017. *National Day Rally Speeches: 50 Years of Nationhood in Singapore (1966–2015)*. Singapore: National Archives of Singapore and Cengage Learning Asia.

Elangovan, Navene. 2021a. "Study Finds 'Clustering' of Races in Some Neighbourhoods Largely Due to Purchasing Power Disparity". *TODAY Online*, 25 July 2021. https://www.todayonline.com/singapore/study-finds-clustering-races-some-neighbourhoods-largely-due-purchasing-power-disparity (accessed 25 July 2021).

———. 2021b. "Teachers Play Key Role in Educating Students to Identify Racism: Panel". *TODAY Online*, 25 June 2021. https://www.todayonline.com/singapore/teachers-play-key-role-educating-students-identify-racism-panellists (accessed 29 July 2021).

Ho, Elaine Lynn-Ee and Foo Fang Yu. 2020. "'New' Chinese Immigrants in Singapore: Localization, Transnational Ties and Integration". In *Navigating Differences: Integration in Singapore*, edited by Terence Chong, pp. 77–90. Singapore: Institute of Southeast Asian Studies.

Ho, Grace. 2021a. "Ceca Does Not Allow Unconditional Entry of Indian PMEs: Ong". *The Straits Times*, 7 July 2021, p. A4.

———. 2021b. "Tighten Salary Criteria, Target Discriminatory Hiring to Ensure Strong S'porean Core: MAS Chief". *The Straits Times*, 15 July 2021, p. B2.

Jalelah, Abu Baker and Lianne Chia. 2020. "GE2020: PAP, PSP, WP and SDP Candidates Take Part in 'Live' General Election Debate". *Channel NewsAsia*, 2 July 2020. https://www.channelnewsasia.com/news/singapore/ge2020-live-broadcast-political-debate-pap-wp-sdp-psp-12891964 (accessed 23 March 2021).

Kathiravelu, Laavanya. 2020. "'What Kind of Indian Are You?': Frictions and Fractures Between Singaporean Indians and Foreign-born NRIs". In *Navigating Differences: Integration in Singapore*, edited by Terence Chong, pp. 110–25. Singapore: Institute of Southeast Asian Studies, 2020.

Lai, Ah Eng. 2012. "Viewing Ourselves and Others: Differences, Disconnects and Divides Among Locals and Immigrants in Singapore". Report Prepared for the CSC-IPS The Population Conundrum – Roundtable on Singapore's Demographic Challenges, 3 May 2012. Singapore: Institute of Policy Studies.

Lam, Fiona and Kelly Ng. 2020. "Singaporeans Hold 43% of Senior Roles in Financial Sector: MAS". *The Business Times*, 19 August 2020. https://www.businesstimes.com.sg/banking-finance/singaporeans-hold-43-of-senior-roles-in-financial-sector-mas (accessed 23 March 2021).

Lim, Min Zhang. 2021. "Iswaran Urges Respect for Different Views on Racial Issues". *The Straits Times*, 18 July 2021, p. A20.

Mathews, Mathew, Melvin Tay, and Shantini Selvarajan. 2019. "Faultlines in Singapore: Public Opinion on Their Realities, Management and Consequences". IPS Working Papers no. 37. Singapore: Institute of Policy Studies.

Mathews, Mathew and Zhang Jiayi. 2016. "Sentiments on Immigrant Integration and the Role of Immigrant Associations". IPS Exchange Series 7. Singapore: Institute of Policy Studies.

Ministry of Education, Singapore. 2015. "Increase in School Fees for Non-citizens in Government and Government-aided Schools from 2016". Press Release, 30 September 2015. https://www.moe.gov.sg/news/press-releases/20150930-increase-in-school-fees-for-non-citizens-in-government-and-government-aided-schools-from-2016 (accessed 10 November 2020).

_____. 2016. "Increase in School Fees for Non-citizens in Government and Government-aided schools from 2017". Press Release, 11 October 2016. https://www.moe.gov.sg/news/press-releases/20161011-increase-in-school-fees-for-non-citizens-in-government-and-government-aided-schools-from-2017 (accessed 10 November 2020).

_____. 2017. "Revised School Fees for Non-citizens in Government and Government-aided Schools from 2018 to 2020". Press Release, 17 October 2017. https://www.moe.gov.sg/news/press-releases/20171017-revised-school-fees-for-non-citizens-in-government-and-government-aided-schools-from-2018-to-2020 (accessed 10 November 2020).

_____. 2018. "Refinements to the Primary One Registration Exercise". Press Release, 20 March 2018". https://www.moe.gov.sg/news/press-releases/20180320-refinements-to-the-primary-one-registration-exercise (accessed 10 November 2020).

_____. 2020a. "2020 Primary One Registration Exercise (For Admission to Primary One in 2021): Updates and New Developments". Press Release, 27 May 2020. https://www.moe.gov.sg/news/press-releases/20200527-2020-primary-one-registration-exercise-for-admission-to-primary-one-in-2021-updates-and-new-developments (accessed 10 November 2020).

———. 2020b. "Full-Paying Foreign Students vs Those Receiving Tuition Grants and Scholarships". Parliamentary Replies, 2 November 2020. https://www.moe.gov.sg/news/parliamentary-replies/20201102-full-paying-foreign-students-vs-those-receiving-tuition-grants-and-scholarships (accessed 10 November 2020).

———. 2021. "Revised School Fees for Non-citizens in Government and Government-aided Schools for 2022 and 2023". Press Release, 21 October 2021. https://www.moe.gov.sg/news/press-releases/20211021-revised-school-fees-for-non-citizens-in-government-and-government-aided-schools-for-2022-and-2023 (accessed 11 April 2021).

Ministry of Manpower. 2021a. "Eligibility for Employment Pass". https://www.mom.gov.sg/passes-and-permits/employment-pass/eligibility (accessed 25 July 2021).

———. 2021b. "Eligibility for S Pass". https://www.mom.gov.sg/passes-and-permits/s-pass/eligibility (accessed 25 July 2021).

Ong, Justin. 2021a. "Foreign Teachers Bring Diversity, Fresh Perspectives". *The Straits Times*, 15 March 2021, p. B4.

———. 2021b. "Number of Teachers From Abroad Has Nearly Halved Since 2011". *The Straits Times*, 15 March 2021, p. B4.

———. 2021c. "Spike in Race, Religion-related Police Reports Last Year". *The Straits Times*, 6 July 2021, p. A8.

Rajah, Indranee. 2021. "Speech by Minister Indranee Rajah on Population at the Committee of Supply Debate 2021". https://www.strategygroup.gov.sg/media-centre/speeches/speech-by-minister-indranee-rajah-on-population-at-the-committee-of-supply-debate-2021 (accessed 23 March 2021).

Tan, Jason. 2010. "Education in Singapore: Sorting Them Out?". In *Management of Success: Singapore Revisited*, edited by Terence Chong, pp. 288–308. Singapore: Institute of Southeast Asian Studies.

Tan, Theresa. 2021. "Singapore's Foreign Brides: 'I Felt So ALONE'". *The Straits Times*, 22 March 2021, p. A6.

Teng, Amelia. 2016a. "More Expats Find It Tough To Get Kids Into Local Schools". *The Sunday Times*, 13 March 2016, p. A12.

———. 2016b. "Rejected, So Expat Families Turn To International Schools". *The Sunday Times*, 13 March 2016, p. A12.

———. 2019. "Home Front: Are Elite Schools Doing Enough To Break Down Barriers?". *The Straits Times*, 31 October 2019. https://www.straitstimes.com/opinion/home-front-are-elite-schools-doing-enough-to-break-down-barriers (accessed 23 March 2021).

———. 2022. "Foreign Students Returning as Border Restrictions Ease". *The Straits Times*, 11 April 2022, p. A3.

Wong, Lawrence. 2021. Speech on Multiracialism and Faultlines by Mr Lawrence Wong, Minister for Finance, at The IPS-RSIS Forum on Race and Racism in Singapore on 25 June 2021. https://www.mof.gov.sg/news-publications/speeches/speech-on-multiracialism-and-faultlines-by-mr-lawrence-wong-minister-for-finance-at-the-ips-rsis-forum-on-race-and-racism-in-singapore-on-25-june-2021 (accessed 29 July 2021).

Yang, Peidong and Chow Lee Tat. 2019. "Immigrant Teachers in Singapore Schools: Backgrounds, Integration, and Diversification". *HSSE Online* 8: 39–51.

Yeoh, Grace. 2021. "Students Who Experience Discrimination 'Should Not Hesitate' to Provide Feedback to Schools: Maliki Osman". *Channel NewsAsia Online*, 5 July 2021. https://www.channelnewsasia.com/news/singapore/students-experience-discrimination-provide-feedback-maliki-osman-15158410 (accessed 25 July 2021).

Zakaria, Mohammed. 2021. "National Junior College Responds to Allegations that Senior Teacher is Racist". https://www.asiaone.com/singapore/national-junior-college-responds-allegations-senior-teacher-racist. *AsiaOne*, 25 June 2021 (accessed 29 July 2021).

7

MANAGING DISASTER RISK AND ENABLING SOCIAL PROTECTION IN THAILAND: SOME LESSONS FROM THE COVID-19 PANDEMIC

Prapaporn Tivayanond Mongkhonvanit

INTRODUCTION

This chapter seeks to examine how Thailand responds to disaster risks. When a disaster strikes and destroys assets and sources of livelihoods, the almost inevitable response of poor households is the use of coping strategies that are harmful to children, to save money on food and to reduce investments in children's health and education. What is required, therefore, is well-designed social protection that can play a key role in enabling households to avoid negative coping strategies and mitigate disaster impact. Disaster-sensitive social protection provides post-disaster relief and rehabilitation that helps households proactively adapt to the threat of natural disasters. By reviewing the contribution of social protection for protecting vulnerable households from the impact of natural disasters, this can contribute to the development of more effective disaster-sensitive social protection programmes in Thailand. This is especially in building household resilience and mitigating disaster risks in scenarios such as the COVID-19 pandemic.

While Thailand has developed a social protection system based on a rights-based approach, that considers different types of risks found in the different generations within the population, past social protection schemes have largely been designed to address normal situations, but not crisis situation. Hence, a mix of both proactive and reactive social protection is necessary in facing the challenges of future risks. The need to expand *functional equivalents* that support livelihood diversification, whilst rendering extensive support for vulnerable people, allows for a complementary approach that addresses not only protection against risks associated with certain events, but for building upon adaptive capacities so that the most vulnerable can sustain their livelihood. In moving forward, assessment of risks needs to consider sudden impacts of change such as those found during a pandemic outbreak or sudden financial crisis. A review of new types of social risks is necessary in the context of expanding the coverage of social protection schemes towards the country's most vulnerable. Furthermore, there is a need to translate resilience objectives into the design of social protection programmes and consider social protection as an important tool in managing risks that can reduce the impact of variability and extremes of new social risks.

FORMS OF SOCIAL PROTECTION

In general, social protection broadly encompasses policies and programmes aimed at preventing, reducing, and eliminating economic and social vulnerabilities to poverty and deprivation (United Nations Children's Fund 2012b). Such policies and programmes play a crucial role in protecting people from risks and hardship and include labour market interventions, social insurance and welfare schemes, social safety nets, and cash or in-kind transfers. Social protection is an important tool to protect populations at risk of falling into poverty as a result of economic or other shocks to their livelihoods. At the same time, it should encourage building household resilience and enabling access to relevant services. Drawing from Devereux and Sabates-Wheeler's (2004) typology, there are two main strands of social protection:

- *Reactive* social protection that is put in place to cope with a major shock or vulnerability (e.g., in response to an earthquake or financial crisis); and
- *Proactive* social protection that aims to invest in people's social security and their ability to manage risks, enables them to plan and be more productive in their livelihood.

The reactive type pertains to protective programmes that offer relief to those with low levels of adaptive capacity through humanitarian support in emergencies and targeted cash transfer schemes. The proactive type includes the following: (1) preventive programmes that avoid damaging coping strategies, particularly before a shock to avert deprivation or to mitigate the impact of an adverse shock. Examples include health and unemployment insurance and non-contributory pension schemes; (2) promotive programmes that enhance resilience through assets, human capital and improving income earning capacity of the poor through skills training and active labour market programmes; (3) transformative interventions that address the underlying causes of power imbalances that create or sustain economic inequality and social exclusion, aimed at transforming social relations. Programmes include legal and judicial reform, budgetary analysis and reform, policy review and monitoring, and social and behavioural change. Overall, these programme types need to be in place to ensure holistic social protection of populations vulnerable to disasters. Preventive programmes, therefore, contribute to risk mitigation before a disaster strikes, while protective programmes that enable coping with a disaster's impact, along with promotive and transformative programmes can reduce risk through facilitating long-term adaptation of livelihood strategies and removal of structural vulnerabilities.

When managing disaster risk, both strands of social protection play an essential role. *Reactive* social protection supports disaster management efforts that include preparedness and response activities. Programmes like cash or in-kind transfers are a common and effective tool to alleviate suffering and support rehabilitation after a disaster strikes. In relation to Disaster Risk Reduction (DRR), *proactive* social protection programmes have the most potential and are increasingly being promoted as an effective and cost-saving tool to build household resilience and avoid the cost of disaster to life, assets, and livelihoods. Programmes such as weather-based crop insurance, employment interventions, and cash transfers can help households to adapt their source of livelihoods and reduce vulnerability. By adapting the targeting criteria and timeframes of existing social protection initiatives—such as cash transfers, employment guarantee schemes and livelihood diversification programmes—disaster-prone and vulnerable groups can benefit at little additional cost.

In addition, it is important to distinguish between contributory and non-contributory social protection. Cash relief that is commonly used for emergency during a natural disaster is classified as non-contributory social protection. Essentially, non-contributory programmes provide benefits to participants without any requirement for financial contribution. These can be universal, categorically targeted, and/or means tested. In Thailand, examples of non-contributory social protection include the Universal Health Coverage programme (universal healthcare) and the State Welfare Card (SWC) Programme. Meanwhile, benefits are provided on the condition that financial contributions are made by or on behalf of beneficiaries. In Thailand, the main contributory social insurance scheme is the Social Security Fund (SSF), under the Social Security Act (Global Extension of Social Security 2013).

Protecting vulnerable population from the impact of natural disasters requires building the resilience of households and communities to withstand natural disasters by preventing and mitigating risk and providing support when a disaster strikes. Social protection plays an important role in different components of disaster risk management (DRM). An increasing body of research confirms the need to integrate social protection and disaster risk reduction. The 2007/8 United Nations' *Human Development Report* called for an expansion of multilateral provisions for countering climate-related humanitarian emergencies and supporting post-disaster recovery, specifying that climate change adaptation should be incorporated into the "post-2012 Kyoto framework and international partnerships for poverty reduction" (Davies et al. 2013, p. 30). Similarly, the World Bank published a review of post-natural disaster interventions, identifying how social protection interventions, such as conditional cash transfers, can reduce vulnerability to extreme disaster impacts at the household level (Fiszbein and Schady 2009).

The purpose of DRM is "to lessen the adverse impacts of hazards and the possibility of disasters" (UNISDR 2009, p. 34) through preventing and mitigating disaster risk and preparing for and responding when a natural disaster strikes. Its two main components are Disaster Risk Reduction (DRR) and Disaster Management (DM). DRR is a proactive approach to managing disaster risk, focused on preventing and mitigating disaster impact. While DRM concentrates on emergency preparedness and disaster response, DRR looks more broadly to address "causal factors of disasters, including through reduced exposure to hazards, lessened vulnerability of people and property, wise management of land and the environment and improved preparedness for adverse events" (UNISDR 2009, p. 20). Many countries in this region have strong mechanisms for disaster management while prevention and mitigation efforts could be further strengthened through comprehensive DRR.

FIGURE 7.1
Disaster Risk Management Classification

Source: United Nations Children's Fund (2012a).

THAILAND AS A CASE STUDY

Thailand is a suitable case study because of its vulnerability to natural disasters and its comparatively advanced social protection mechanisms found within the Southeast Asian region. It also allows us to contextualize answers to the following questions:

- How are existing social protection programmes supporting both disaster response and rehabilitation (reactive programmes); and disaster risk mitigation and prevention (proactive)?
- What are the opportunities and challenges for strengthening the linkage between social protection and disaster risk management?

- How does the lesson of the existing social protection scheme in disaster translate to a wider implication of protection against other risk scenarios such as the COVID-19 pandemic?

A desk review of government and academic publications as well as reports by development organizations was conducted, along with reviews of data on Thai local communities affected by a natural disaster, such as the widespread flooding in 2011 that hit 65 provinces in Thailand (Thailand Department of Disaster Prevention and Mitigation 2012). This was also complemented by semi-structured interviews with key counterparts in relevant ministries and development partners such as the Ministry of the Interior, the Ministry of Natural Resources and Environment, and the Ministry of Social Development and Human Security in Thailand.

In the past decade, Thailand has been affected by a number of natural disasters, notably the 2004 Indian Ocean Tsunami that cost thousands of lives and severe flooding in 2011–12. Hence, the recent emergence of social protection in Thailand outlines the existing DRM framework, and explores the disaster-sensitivity of existing social protection programmes. It reveals that DRM in Thailand is, to a large extent, focused on response and rehabilitation and that there is scope to increase efforts for DRR. Examples of disaster-sensitive social protection schemes exist, like the "One Tambon One Product" scheme for livelihood diversification. It suggests that there is political will to strengthen the linkage between social protection and DRR that is often not made explicit and appears incidental.

Thai children and their families are highly vulnerable to natural disasters. Severe droughts and floods are a threat to life, assets, and livelihoods, particularly in the central, eastern, and southern regions, and are becoming more frequent and intense with climate change (Marks 2011). Between 2000 and 2009, three droughts caused an estimated damage of US$422 million (CRED EM-DAT 2012). Between 2002 and 2010, floods led to over US$1.2 billion of damage and economic losses (Rernirungsathit 2011) to people's livelihoods. In 2004, Thailand was also seriously affected by the Indian Ocean Tsunami and the flooding that followed, resulting in an estimated 8,200 deaths (Schwartz et al. 2006). Severe flooding in 2011 along the Mekong and Chao Phraya River basins, through the provinces of northern, north-eastern and central Thailand affected approximately 13.6 million people (*The Nation* 2011).

The World Bank estimates the cost of economic damage at US$45.7 billion (World Bank 2009).

Poorer households are most vulnerable to disaster impact. During the 2011 floods, household income was found to be a major factor for disaster preparedness, with high-income households more able to protect themselves against risks (National Statistics Office 2011). This underlines the need for social protection to support the poorest and build their resilience to withstand disaster impact and avoid coping mechanisms that are harmful to children. To place in this context, Thailand has a population of 69.7 million people, of whom 17 per cent are under the age of 15, and has a rapidly ageing population, with 11 per cent of the population aged 65 or over (World Bank 2016). In addition, the evolution of social protection in Thailand can be explained by looking at the situation prior to the 1997 Asian financial crisis compared with that following the 2008 global economic crisis. Understanding the origin of social protection will help to explain the incidental nature of the linkages between social protection, DRM and climate change adaptation.

The 1997 crisis was instrumental in the formation of the current structure. Before the crisis, Thailand's economy was characterized by export-led economic growth. The prioritization of export-oriented economic development meant that social protection mainly covered the formal sector of civil servants and large corporations (e.g., civil servant pension scheme, social security fund and provident fund offered by corporations), while there was an absence of protection for the informal sector. The loss of income and unemployment among workers in the rural economy resulting from the crisis heightened the effects of the lack of social protection. There is a need to increase coverage of informal workers and their families (76 per cent of the total population) through the provision of rights-based and adequate protection against poverty for all citizens, especially vulnerable groups such as children, the elderly, and the disabled.

Despite the progression of Thailand's social protection scheme following the 1997 financial crisis, the voluntary nature of the Social Security Act under Article 40 has left many of the most vulnerable still vulnerable. Many have not accessed the national social security provision due to access problems. Social security covers only private companies that are registered with the Ministry of Commerce. It fails to cover those who do not belong to the formal labour market, such

TABLE 7.1
Social Protection Schemes (pre-1997 and post-2008)

Coverage	Pre-1997 Crisis	Post-1997 Asian Financial Crisis	Post-2008 Global Economic Crisis
Formal Sector: Private & Government Sectors (Thailand Department of Labour Protection and Welfare 1999)	• Provident Fund • Civil Servants' Pension Scheme • Social Security Fund	• Provident Fund • Civil Servants' Pension Scheme • Social Security Fund	• Provident Fund • Civil Servants' Pension Scheme • Social Security Fund
Informal sector and non-government sector	Social Security Act 1990: Benefits covering sickness, disability, death, childbirth, old age, and child welfare. (Unemployment benefit was drafted in the Social Security Act, but it was not provided.) • Labour Protection Act 1998 • Workmen's Compensation Fund (Thailand Department of Labour Protection and Welfare 1999) • Severance Pay (Thailand Department of Labour Protection and Welfare, 1999) • Provident Fund (Thailand Department of Labour Protection and Welfare, 1999) • Employee Welfare Fund (Thailand Department of Labour Protection and Welfare, 1999)	Additional schemes: Dual Track Policies: • "One Tambon One Product" (OTOP) • Village and Urban Revolving Fund (T.F.J. 2013) • Three-year debt moratorium • Small and Medium Enterprise Bank • 30 Baht Health Scheme	Additional schemes: • Universal tax-financed US$18 (THB500) as income security for elderly over 60 years. • Revision of Social Security Act, Article 40 of voluntary package covering sickness, invalidity, death, and old-age pension (lump sum amount) (Rernirungsathit 2013). • National Savings Fund for Thais aged 15–60. Members have to contribute monthly. Depending on the amount contributed (ceiling of US$18 or THB600) and age, members will benefit from a contribution from the government (Global Extension of Social Security 2013).

Source: Author's own compilation from documentary data and interviews.

as self-employed small business workers, unpaid family workers, farmers, etc.

It is also important to note that many of the country's social protection schemes are not able to reduce exposure to social risks given that the average expenditure per person in social protection that the government subsidizes is still less than the poverty line. Non-contributory benefits (mainly unconditional cash transfers) cover only a small part of the minimum expenditures required to meet beneficiaries' basic needs: they account for one-tenth to one-fifth of the average incomes of their target population, and represent around a quarter to a third of the value of relevant regional poverty lines. Furthermore, the low level of non-contributory benefits is particularly challenging for those unable to work.

MAPPING DISASTER AND SOCIAL PROTECTION PROGRAMMES

Social protection in Thailand is contributing to efforts to manage disaster risk. The incidental linkage between social protection and disaster risk could be strengthened by intensifying DRR programmes that are integrated with proactive social protection programmes. The weather-based crop insurance and the One Tambon One Product (OTOP) livelihood diversification scheme are examples of programmes that can help affected populations avoid coping strategies harmful to children. The programmes' impact on disaster risk is limited because programme design and implementation are not explicitly geared towards disaster sensitivity.

Any significant linkages between programmes and outcome for now are mostly incidental and there is great potential to strengthen DRM by adjusting programmes to cover disaster-affected populations, particularly the poorest who are most vulnerable to disaster and climate change impact. A preliminary case study of the 2011 Thai floods suggests that existing reactive social protection in emergencies (especially cash transfers) needs to be reformed to remove delays in disbursement of assistance and facilitate more proactive efforts to reduce disaster risk.

In previous cases of disasters in Thailand, one finds that under *protective* and *preventative* coping strategies, social protection services such as the 30 Baht health scheme or free education for all children from pre-school to high school, were not specifically aimed at citizens with low levels of adaptive capacity (Davies 2009). Meanwhile, strategies that aimed to build adaptive capacities and to promote resilience through livelihood diversification and security, such as basic social transfers or even access to credit via public bank, were limited, to the extent that there are still abundant informal loans found in the system. As a result, informal debts are increasingly becoming a serious problem among workers in urban areas as substantial numbers of the workforce lack access to proper sources of capital (*Bangkok Post* 2012). Some of these strategies are as follows:

(A) Limiting Income Risks: Weather-indexed Crop Insurance

The weather-indexed insurance for rice was introduced in 2008 and provides payments to insured farmers based on indices of rainfall or temperature from weather stations. These payments equalize income losses that may otherwise lead to coping strategies such as reducing expenditure on food, health, and education, undermining children's opportunity to thrive. Farmers are able to claim US$19 per 0.16 hectares (THB606 per rai). The insurance scheme has a direct link to disaster risk and climate change and reduces the personal risk to farmers stemming from crop failures and incentivizes adapting agricultural practices to the effects of climate change. During the 2011 floods, an estimated 65,600 hectares (410,000 rai) of rice growing land was submerged by flood waters, with a total loss of US$180 million (THB5.7 billion) (Ayutthaya Provincial Public Disaster Prevention and Mitigation Office 2012). The scheme helped farmers who were unable to access official government assistance. Its coverage, however, is limited by the affordability of insurance premiums. This is especially in the case of poorer farmers in high-risk areas who are unable to afford the premiums. The scheme should be adapted to enable all farmers to access the insurance and protect children from disaster or climate change impacts (World Bank 2009).

(B) Livelihood Diversification: One Tambon One Product (OTOP) Scheme

The OTOP policy was introduced in 2001 to create jobs in agricultural areas, keep farmers on their farms, improve their incomes, and reduce household debt. The policy encourages local entrepreneurship by supporting communities in developing and selling localized products (e.g., handicrafts, cotton and silk garments, pottery and household and food items). The government provides a local and international stage for the promotion of these products (rather than financial support). The scheme raises disposable household income with benefits for spending on children, especially given its benefits for women producers who are able to work from home and earn income. This is particularly so in rural areas, where natural disasters like floods can remove a household's only source of income by destroying crops. In this case, alternative income sources are key to enable households to avoid coping mechanisms harmful to children. OTOP is a scheme that can contribute to livelihood diversification, multiplying sources of income, and increasing household resilience.

FIGURE 7.2
One Tambon One Product Household Financial Use

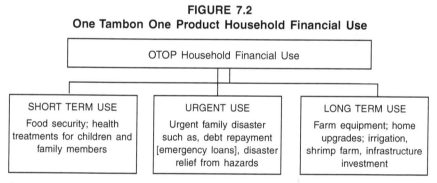

Source: Analysis from documentary data and interviews with OTOP producers. Twenty-eight interviews were undertaken with OTOP producers at the OTOP Annual Fair 2010.

(C) Universalizing Health Care: 30 Baht Health Scheme

The 30 Baht health scheme, launched in 2001, is an ambitious universal coverage scheme that provides an annual lump sum per-patient subsidy to all hospitals and limits co-payment of patients to THB30 Baht per hospital visit. It increased health care utilization, especially by children and elderly. Among the less fortunate living in precarity, it significantly reduced infant mortality rates in poorer provinces (prior to the scheme, poorer provinces had higher infant mortality rates than the wealthier provinces). The scheme has reduced the cost of public healthcare—particularly for children with illnesses and women of childbearing age—from an average of THB500 per household per year to THB30 per hospital visit (Gruber et al. 2013). While there is no explicit link to disaster risk, the universal removal of access barriers enables populations affected by disasters to seek medical treatment without having to rely on emergency assistance that may be delayed by time-consuming administrative procedures (as described in the case study above). Nevertheless, the main challenge to ensuring universal health care access is limitations in staff availability in rural areas.

(D) Cash Transfers during the 2011 Floods in Thailand

Social protection programmes like cash or in-kind transfers are also vital components of disaster response and rehabilitation. Cash transfer or non-contributory scheme assists people during the initial stage of the disaster aftermath. It is a top-down, general provision of cash, which can be dispensed expediently to affected communities. The main challenge of providing these emergency transfers to disaster victims is the lengthy procedures necessary to verify who is affected and entitled to assistance. In contrast, proactive disaster-sensitive social protection programmes, already in place before a disaster strikes, can provide timely support to those affected by scaling up support in case of an emergency. Social protection programmes offer relief and support during the crisis, as community members were able to utilize additional income sources to address direct and indirect risks from flooding.

PROTECTION PROGRAMMES DURING THE COVID-19 PANDEMIC

The Thai government was one of the first in the region to implement a wide range of emergency social protection responses during the initial outbreak of the COVID-19 pandemic from 2020. As part of ad-hoc relief, measures included a one-off cash assistance of US$150 (5,000 Thai Baht) for three months to informal sector workers and farmers affected by COVID-19 (Ariyapruchya et al. 2020). Cash handouts are, however, insufficient to mitigate the impact of income lost as they exclude some vulnerable groups due to eligibility criteria.

Given the high share of informal employment and a large number of smaller enterprises and family businesses, COVID-19 has had a disproportionately negative impact on the poor and those who belong to the lower part of Thailand's workforce—these are the people most vulnerable due to their lack of regular income and productive assets.

Challenges abound in reaching out to these most vulnerable groups. The Thai government reported 27 million people applied online for the cash handout. But by April 2021, only 1.68 million of them have been approved (Ariyapruchya et al. 2020). In order to apply for the income support, one has to have access to the internet and hold a saving account. This requirement has excluded some from the poorest communities such as daily wage workers, street vendors, and taxi drivers. Similar to scenarios arising from a natural disaster, those belonging to informal sectors, such as street vendors, have been the hardest hit in Thailand.

It is for this reason that the Thai government was able to achieve more impact by using the existing social protection system as an insertion to support its people. The impact was felt when the government expanded on existing social security schemes under the Social Security Fund, and these have provided support to enterprises and protection for workers and their families. The recent government decision to provide emergency top-up funding to beneficiaries of the Child Support Grant, Disability Grant, Old Age Allowance and the State Welfare Card was an important addition. By building on existing social protection schemes, the monthly top-up of 1,000 baht for three months provided additional economic support to many vulnerable families severely affected by COVID-19.

Nonetheless, more than half of workers in Thailand are informal, meaning they are not covered by a social security scheme and are particularly vulnerable. Assistance did not reach these people. During the height of the COVID-19 pandemic, it was estimated that more than 20 million workers are part of the informal sector. Moreover, families with children who were not identified as vulnerable were not eligible to receive the Child Support Grant (CSG) (Davin and Buckley 2020). The gap in the social protection system in Thailand, therefore, remains especially salient for the informal sector and the most vulnerable. For this reason, there is a systematic need for the Thai government to make sure that particularly vulnerable groups, including migrants, older people, and pregnant women are protected.

LESSONS FROM THE COVID-19 PANDEMIC FOR BETTER SOCIAL PROTECTION

With reference to what has been discussed in relation to disaster risk reduction and disaster risk management, lessons from the COVID-19 pandemic greatly reveals the need to adapt instruments to new circumstances. This is largely due to restrictive intervention patterns in addressing immediate risk whenever situations like disasters or pandemics arise. Social protection plays a very important role as a specific risk management tool and should be better facilitated in future challenges. The case of Thailand shows that a disaster sensitive social protection in the country can be limited by institutional frameworks. This is because such frameworks do not sufficiently integrate social protection into DRM policies and plans. The result is that linkages often appear incidental and that synergies are not used to their maximum potential. Thailand needs to make social protection move towards a more integrated approach.

The impact of the COVID-19 pandemic created an opportunity to rethink the traditional foundations of social protection policy in Thailand. There is a need for social protection system to suit the changing nature of work and an economy with high rates of the informality of Thailand. It should also meet the needs of the most vulnerable, while ensuring fiscal sustainability, and be adjustable to respond quickly to threats like the pandemics. More priority should be directed towards strengthening national systems for responding to natural disasters and preventing and mitigating the risk they pose for children and their families. This requires concerted efforts by national governments and development partners to identify programmes and policies that work. In the case of Thailand, there is potential for the construction of exemplary disaster sensitive social protection programmes. One key starting point is to identify opportunities in order to further strengthen and intensify efforts at managing emerging risks. The following are proposed:

(A) The Need for Both Reactive and Proactive Social Protection

Cash and in-kind transfers are an important component of post-disaster relief and rehabilitation efforts. It can take time until assistance programmes triggered by disasters are fully operational and help reaches victims. Making sure that existing social protection programmes are disaster-sensitive makes it easy to scale-up assistance when a disaster strikes and help affected populations without delay. This requires adapting targeting criteria to focus on populations at risk of disasters of any kind, especially the poorest and most vulnerable.

(B) Functional Equivalents during the COVID-19 Pandemic

Social protection in disaster response and rehabilitation efforts include cash transfers and cash-for-work programmes for victims and are complemented by modified social protection programmes with a broad focus on poverty reduction. Disaster and climate change risks are mitigated by programmes that enable those vulnerable to disasters to find alternative sources of income (livelihood diversification) and disaster-resilient housing. Thailand's One Tambon One Product scheme supports small-scale farmers to develop additional sources of income, mitigating the risk of lack of income when a disaster destroys agricultural crops. Such schemes can help households secure alternative sources of income, reducing their vulnerability to income losses caused by natural disasters.

Schemes that build household resilience and making existing programmes more disaster-sensitive should be expanded, so it will ensure that the poorest in society who face the worst disaster risks are targeted and not excluded by barriers such as high premiums. Herein, extensive support for vulnerable people is couched in existing policies or functional equivalents that target the informal sector in the first place. These functional equivalents include providing employment subsidies and building on initial measures to make unemployment insurance system more generous. Other policies include reskilling and upskilling measures for unemployed workers. In response to the COVID-19 pandemic, the Thai government needs to consider integrating support with existing policies or functional equivalents that target the informal sector in the first place.

(C) Expanding Coverage of Social Protection Benefit

The COVID-19 pandemic has underscored challenges faced by workers in the informal sector. The 5,000-baht scheme allowed for an unprecedented registration of these workers. It is time for the Thai government to develop an integrated strategy to promote the formalization of workers and businesses, including registering workers under social security schemes. These could include making contributions portable across Social Security Funding Articles in order to accommodate varied employment histories and prevent disincentives to participation. Moreover, the families of those who belong to the informal sector include children and women. There is a need to increase coverage and adequacy of social protection for children, especially poor children aged 0–17 and pregnant women. These can further include expansion of non-contributory assistance in the form of the child support grant.

(D) Increasing Universalization of Social Protection (Dankmeyer 2019)

Over time, the Thai government needs to consider establishing programmes with universal benefits to help cushion epidemic outbreaks that may occur in the medium term as well as other negative shocks, complemented by more programmes for the most vulnerable. Thailand will therefore need better targeting mechanisms. A universal Child Support Grant, for example, would protect children in the face of any future economic or environmental crises and reduce the risk of families in need of being left without financial support.

(E) A Focus on Resilience Building Under Social Protection

Social protection has a role to play to support victims after a disaster strikes. But it also has the potential to reduce the impact of disasters by supporting risk mitigation and prevention efforts. Proactively reducing risk by supporting households relocate away from areas vulnerable to disasters and diversify their source of livelihood can save lives and avoid much larger costs of reconstruction and rehabilitation after a disaster strikes. Based on the review cited earlier, there are limited examples of comprehensive risk mitigation and prevention programmes that incorporated social protection. This underlines the need to strengthen proactive elements of national programmes to manage risk coupled with a stronger focus on proactive, social protection to build the resilience of households in Thailand.

Expectations of what single social protection programmes can or cannot do to build resilience need to be realistic, particularly in terms of the timeframes required to build programmes' capacity to deliver outputs well. It is, then, not just about natural disasters or pandemics. Vulnerability is multidimensional and households are exposed to a range of risks that go beyond natural disaster shocks. Programmes that aim to build resilience need to apply a comprehensive approach to reducing risks, which include slow-onset changes related to social, economic and health risks.

One must recall that social protection is fundamentally a tool for resilience, and consequently, social protection programmes are becoming popular tools to help people cope with all kinds of shocks and stresses. The rising challenges of different kinds of risks, such as natural disaster and disease, increasingly require policymakers to put in place programmes that enhance resilience and ensure efforts to reduce vulnerability and inequality. To have an impact, there is a need to translate resilience objectives into the design of social protection programmes.

In terms of resilience-building in light of the COVID-19 pandemic, there is a need to underpin variations in resilience capacities. Social protection programmes need to be laid down to cope with variability and extremes during and after a disturbance to reduce the immediate impact on people's livelihoods and basic needs. This pertains to national programmes that make a strong contribution to people's capacities to absorb the negative impacts of related shocks and stresses on their livelihoods. They do so through the provision of well-implemented, regular cash transfers—regardless of whether these are aimed specifically to address lifecycle-based risks. At the same time, there is a need for social systems to actively anticipate and reduce the impact of variability and extremes through preparedness and planning. Even general programmes such as social pensions, for example, should present indications of preparedness for disaster shocks at the household level.

Finally, social systems need to adapt to multiple, long-term and future risks, and also to learn and adjust after a disaster. While adaptation does not necessarily have to be an explicit objective of social protection programmes, contributions to adaptive capacity can potentially come from linkages with programmes that aim to build sustainable livelihoods. Our understanding of all these capacities will be necessary, especially as the forms and different dimensions of risks, as well as social protection evolve in our society today.

REFERENCES

Ariyapruchya, Kiatipong, Arvind Nair, Judy Yang, and Harry Edmund Moroz. 2020. "The Thai Economy: Covid 19, Poverty, and Social Protection". World Bank. https://blogs.worldbank.org/eastasiapacific/thai-economy-covid-19-poverty-and-social-protection.

Ayutthaya Provincial Public Disaster Prevention and Mitigation Office. 2012. "Ayutthaya Action Plan for Flood". Ayutthaya Disaster Prevention and Mitigation Department.

Bangkok Post. 2012. "Poor Thais Trapped in Informal Debts", 18 December 2012. https://www.bangkokpost.com/thailand/politics/326792/thai-industrial-workers-trapped-by-informal-debts.

CRED EM-DAT database. 2012. "The International Disaster Database". Brussels: Centre for Research on the Epidemiology of Disaster (CRED). http://www.mdat.be/database.

Dankmeyer, Christina. 2019. "Universal Social Protection: What It Means and Why It Concerns All of Us". Socialprotection.org. https://socialprotection.org/discover/blog/universal-social-protection-what-it-means-and-why-it-concerns-all-us.

Davies, Mark, Christophe Béné, Alexander Arnall, Thomas Tanner, Andrew J. Newsham, and Cristina Coirolo. 2013. "Promoting Resilient Livelihoods through Adaptive Social Protection: Lessons from 124 Programmes in South Asia". *Development Policy Review* 31, no. 1: 27–58.

Davin, Thomas and Graeme Buckley. 2020. "Social Protection is Pathway to Pandemic Recovery". Unicef. https://www.unicef.org/thailand/stories/social-protection-pathway-pandemic-recovery.

Devereux, Stephen and Rachel Sabates-Wheeler. 2004. "Transformative Social Protection". IDS Working Paper 232. Brighton: Institute of Development Studies.

Fiszbein, Ariel and Norbert Schady. 2009. *Conditional Cash Transfers: Reducing Present and Future Poverty*. World Bank.

Global Extension of Social Security. 2013. "Thailand Country Profile". http://www.social-protection.org/gimi/gess/ShowCountryProfile.do?cid=404.

Gruber, Jonathan, Nathaniel Henderen, and Robert M. Towsend. 2013. "The Great Equalizer: Health Care Access and Infant Mortality in Thailand". Cambridge: MIT Department of Economics.

Guhan, Sanjivi. 1994. "Social Security Options for Developing Countries". *International Labour Review* 133, no. 1: 35–53.

Marks, Danny. 2011. "Climate Change and Thailand: Impact and Responses". *Contemporary Southeast Asia* 33, no. 2: 229–58.

National Statistical Office (NSO) and the Health Systems Research Institute and Emergency Medicine Institute. 2011. http://kb.hsri.or.th/dspace/select-purpose/11228/3503/3/hsri-annual2011.pdf.

Rernirungsathit, Phatsita. 2011. "Thailand: Country Profiles 2011". Bangkok: ADRC. www.adrc.asia/countryreport/THA/2011/FY2011B_THA_CR.pdf.

Schwartz, Dagan, Avishay Goldberg, Issac Ashkenasi, Guy Nakash, Rami Pelts, Adi Leiba, Yeheskel Levi, and Yaron Bar-Dayan. 2006. "Prehospital Care of Tsunami Victims in Thailand: Description and Analysis". *Pre-hospital Disaster Medicine* 21, no. 3: 204–10.

T.F.J. 2013. "The Biggest Microlender of them all". *The Economist*, January 2013. https://www.economist.com/schumpeter/2013/01/01/the-biggest-microlender-of-them-all.

Thailand Department of Disaster Prevention and Mitigation. 2010. "National Disaster Risk Reduction Strategic Action Plan (B.E. 2553-2562)". Bangkok: Ministry of the Interior. http://www.disaster.go.th/dpm/index.php?option=com_docman&itemid=221.

──────. 2012. "Public Disaster Prevention Act". Bangkok: Ministry of the Interior.

Thailand Department of Labour Protection and Welfare. 1999. "Labour Protection Act 1998". Bangkok: Ministry of Labour and Social Welfare. http://www.aseanhrmech.org/downloads/Thailand-Labor_Protection_Act_of_1998.pdf.

The Nation. 2011. "Floodings in Bang Bua Thong, Pak Kret Hits Critical Levels", 21 October 2011.

United Nations Children's Fund. 2012a. "Child-Centered Disaster Risk Reduction – Guidance Notes for UNICEF Asia-Pacific". Bangkok: UNICEF East Asia and Pacific Regional Office.

──────. 2012b. *Integrated Social Protection Systems: Enhancing Equity for Children*. New York: UNICEF. www.unicef.org/socialprotection/framework.

United Nations Development Programme. 2008. "Climate Shocks: Risk and Vulnerability in an Unequal World". *Human Development Report 2007/2008*. New York: United Nations Development Programme.

United Nations Institute Strategy for Disaster Reduction (UNISDR). 2009. *Terminology on Disaster Risk Reduction*.

United Nations Office for Disaster Risk Reduction. 2008. *Hyogo Framework for Action 2005-2015: Building the Resilience of Nations and Communities to Disasters*. Geneva: United Nations Office for Disaster Risk Reduction. https://www.unisdr.org/2005/wcdr/intergover/official-doc/L-docs/Hyogo-framework-for-action-english.pdf.

World Bank. 2009. *Assessment of Innovative Approaches to Flood Risk Management and Financing in Agriculture: The Thailand Case Study*. World Bank.

──────. 2016. *Thailand Economic Monitor – June 2016: Aging Society and Economy*. https://www.worldbank.org/en/country/thailand/publication/thailand-economic-monitor-june-2016-aging-society-and-economy.

8

TRANSNATIONAL HOUSING INSECURITY: MOBILITY, HOMELESSNESS, AND THE COVID-19 PANDEMIC

Kok-Hoe Ng and Jeyda Simren Sekhon Atac

Transnational migrants are vulnerable to homelessness and form a large proportion of the homeless population in many places (Crisis 2021; Parliament of Victoria 2021; Pleace 2010; Smith 2018, 2019). Their housing insecurity is associated with barriers to work, housing and welfare (Amundson 2017; Daly 1996; Djuve et al. 2015; Fitzpatrick et al. 2015; Mostowska 2013). They are often excluded from the formal labour market due to limited rights to work and restricted to the least desirable housing options because of the precarity of informal work. Access to housing and other welfare services is further hindered by poor understanding of local practices, language and bureaucratic barriers, and fear of repatriation or deportation. Most of the literature is concerned with the housing experiences of refugees and asylum seekers (Smith 2018), or labour migrants who relocate for economic reasons, instead of highly mobile transnational persons who make frequent and repeated border crossings (for exceptions, see Campbell and Lachica 2013; Järv et al. 2021).

During the COVID-19 pandemic, homelessness spiked in many countries due to an increase in unemployment, poverty and evictions (Benavides and Nukpezah 2020; Benfer et al. 2021). Persons sleeping in public spaces faced greater exposure to infection and other physical and mental health risks (Udechukwu et al. 2021; Wang et al. 2021). In response, governments introduced emergency food and shelter services; stepped up outreach, rental assistance and temporary housing; suspended evictions; distributed personal hygiene items; and provided health and safety information (Fitzpatrick et al. 2020; Honorato and Oliviera 2020; Kelleher and Norris 2020; OECD 2021; Parsell et al. 2020; Wilczek 2020). The impact of the pandemic was heightened for economically marginalized labour migrants whose livelihoods were disrupted by travel restrictions (Shahare 2021). While refugees were targeted with stricter lockdown measures in some cases (Spyratou 2020), governments in places like the United Kingdom and Germany lifted rules that normally excluded migrants from accessing housing and welfare support (Barbu et al. 2021).

In Southeast Asia, the pandemic also affected migration and transnational populations. Within the region, migrants typically move from Myanmar to Thailand, from Indonesia to Malaysia, and from Malaysia to Singapore (Lian et al. 2016). The corridor between Singapore, Malaysia and Indonesia sees particularly heavy migration flows (Testaverde et al. 2017). A recent report estimated that "more than 300,000 Malaysians travel across the Johor-Singapore Causeway every day, making it one of the busiest overland border crossings in the region" (CNA 2018). Border closures introduced in March and April 2020 severely disrupted these linkages. Singapore closed its borders to visitors and issued advisories to citizens against international travel (Ministry of Health 2020a, 2020b, 2020c). Persons who disregarded the advice had to bear the costs of COVID-19 tests and quarantine—otherwise provided free-of-charge—upon their return. Indonesia similarly advised citizens against leaving the country and suspended the entry of foreign visitors (Acting Director General of Immigration 2020; Directorate General of Immigration 2020). Malaysia imposed a Movement Control Order (MCO) that barred citizens from leaving and foreigners from entry (CNA 2020).

Media attention was focused on Malaysians who lived in the southernmost state of Johor and usually commuted to Singapore for work (Meah 2021; Yusof 2020). Up to 250,000 Malaysians were estimated to be in this category (Rahman 2021). After travel was stopped by border closures, those who returned to Malaysia struggled to find new livelihoods, as Johor's economy was tightly linked to business and tourist flows from Singapore. Others who chose to stay in Singapore had to find accommodation and deal with long-term separation from their families. There were only isolated accounts of Singaporeans who used to live in Malaysia or Indonesia, and became homeless after they returned to Singapore to wait out the lockdown (Chia 2021; Harris and Campbell 2021).

As a global city of a developmental mould (Sassen 2002; Tai 2006; Ye and Kelly 2011), Singapore carefully plans and tightly manages migration flows to its economic advantage, while keeping an eye on their possible impact on social harmony and national identity (Montsion 2012; Yeoh and Chang 2001). The state's overall strategy has firstly been to export "cosmopolitan" citizens to take advantage of opportunities in the global economy, and secondly to select and import foreign nationals sorted into high- and low-skill categories, or "foreign talent" versus "foreign workers" in local discourse (Yeoh 2006). Professionals and elites are recruited mainly in service of Singapore's thriving financial sectors (Beaverstock 2002; Hof 2019; Lam et al. 2002; Zhan et al. 2020). Their voluntary mobility contrasts with the enforced transience of foreign workers found in occupations such as domestic and construction work, who are brought in on a "use and discard" basis (Yeoh and Chang 2001, p. 1032). Public policy excludes this second group from the employment and wage protections accorded to nationals, polices their use of public spaces, segregates their housing from local neighbourhoods, and prohibits migration with family and marriage with Singaporeans (Goh 2019; Kaur 2006; Yeoh et al. 2017).

Past research has highlighted in-migration from low-cost societies such as Malaysia to high-wage economies like Singapore (Ho and Tyson 2011; Lam et al. 2002; Rizzo and Glasson 2011). In contrast, the out-migration of economically disadvantaged Singaporeans to neighbouring Malaysia and Indonesia has received far less attention. Before COVID-19, the Johor-Singapore Community Care Association estimated that 5,000 Singaporean families lived in Johor (Oh and Jagtiani 2016). Many moved to Malaysia as a lifestyle choice. As they worked in Singapore and lived in Johor, they enjoyed "both Malaysia's cheaper cost of living and Singapore's higher purchasing power" (Ho and Tyson 2011, p. 137). Border crossing gave them access to "a middle-class life", including homeownership, for "half of what they cost in Singapore" (Oh and Jagtiani 2016, p. 277). Another reason is retirement. A growing transnational retirement industry in the region allows older Singaporeans to access affordable residential care facilities in Johor (Ormond 2014; Tai and Toh 2015; Toyota and Xiang 2012). Khamsya's (2016) fieldwork revealed a group of older Singaporean Malays who retired in villages in Johor where they practised a form of transnational householding, maintaining their ties with family in Singapore while enjoying local community life and social support. Some of them even purchased low-cost social housing meant for Malaysians through local proxies.

As for Indonesia, research has mainly been concerned with Singaporeans in Batam, the largest city in the Riau Islands that has longstanding economic relations with Singapore and is only a short distance away. Recent research estimated that 300 to 500 Singaporeans lived in Batam (Oh and Jagtiani 2016). They fall into two categories. The first are managers and entrepreneurs, usually men, who are deployed by their Singapore-based companies or have set up their own businesses in Batam. Their stays are usually short-term and they make weekly trips back to Singapore to visit family. The second group of Singaporean migrants are married to Indonesians. These are often "men who are increasingly marginalised in the globalising economy [and] become involved with less well-off women from the other side of the border" (Amster and Lindquist 2005, p. 3).

This study focuses on highly mobile Singaporeans who live in Malaysia and Indonesia but travel frequently back to Singapore. Some of them had set up home with their family overseas, so did not have housing in Singapore. Others could not afford to purchase housing or encountered barriers in the social housing system. Through their individual narratives, it examines how the causes, conditions and context of transnational mobility contributed to housing insecurity during the COVID-19 pandemic. Housing insecurity is defined as the lack of stable and adequate housing, and includes homelessness. Empirically, knowledge of this group of migrants is still limited. An analysis of their circumstances can aid theoretical understanding of the housing insecurity associated specifically with mobility, as distinct from migration for the purposes of permanent relocation. It can also contribute to a fuller picture of actual migration practices in a global city, beyond state-orchestrated strategies. The study will address three related questions: How do Singaporean migrants in Malaysia and Indonesia manage social ties, economic needs and institutional barriers? How does their mobility produce housing insecurity and when does this tip over into street homelessness? How much of the observed phenomenon may be considered an acute, temporary reaction to the pandemic, and how much is part of a long-term pattern? The following sections will present the study method and findings, before summarizing the response to these questions and considering the implications for policy and research.

METHOD

In April 2020, when Singapore entered its COVID-19 lockdown, known locally as the "circuit breaker", a homelessness outreach group issued an unprecedented call for businesses, NGOs and families to open their premises to rough sleepers, as existing shelters had reached capacity. Rough sleeping refers to sleeping in places not meant for human habitation (Busch-Geertsema et al. 2015). A press report suggested that "thousands" needed help (Liu 2020). By the end of the month, the government had mobilized a network of religious groups to provide temporary shelter to a growing number of homeless people. At its peak, the network had 35 organizations that could house 700 people (Goh 2020). This surge in shelter demand had a longer backdrop. A study published shortly before the start of COVID-19 found that there were between 921 and 1,050 rough sleepers in Singapore (Ng 2019). Job and income losses triggered by the pandemic, as well as border closures stranding the transnational population, would likely have increased this number. Restrictions on access to public spaces during the lockdown then compelled homeless people to seek shelter.

This study took place on the crest of these developments, when opportunity arose to interview residents from one of the temporary shelters in late 2020 and early 2021. The interviews were part of a larger study that included a nationwide street count (Ng and Sekhon Atac 2022). In total, 51 participants were interviewed. They were initially recruited with the help of social workers and later through snowballing. As this is a hard-to-reach population, and there has been no published research on shelter residents in Singapore to the authors' best knowledge, no other filters were applied and all residents who agreed to take part were accepted for the interviews. Their accounts depict an important dimension of housing insecurity in Singapore but are not necessarily representative of all homeless people. The participants are considered homeless since shelters are not a permanent place of residence. A distinction is normally drawn in housing research between sheltered homeless and street homeless persons, with the terms street homelessness and rough sleeping used interchangeably (Busch-Geertsema et al. 2015). Whether these shelter residents had been rough sleeping before the pandemic was in fact one of the empirical questions the study was interested in.

This chapter focuses on the 22 interviewees who were transnational, that is, living in Malaysia or Indonesia before the pandemic struck. Half of them had experiences of rough sleeping. As shown in Table 8.1, most of them were male, aged 50 years and above, and Singapore citizens. Their educational level was fairly low—there was only one diploma holder among them—a constraint that affected their employment opportunities. Half of them were not married but the majority had family members living outside Singapore. Overall, the gender, age, marital, employment and educational profile of the participants is very similar to that of the larger street homeless population in Singapore (Ng 2019).

The semi-structured interviews were conducted by three researchers, including the authors. They followed the same interview guide, which consisted of a list of mainly open-ended questions on topics such as the participants' family and economic situations, housing histories, and experiences of rough sleeping and shelter living. Each interview lasted around 60 minutes and happened in-person at a public place, usually a shopping mall food-court or fast-food restaurant. Interviews were audio recorded and later transcribed in full. Most interviews were conducted in English. A few Mandarin interviews were first transcribed before translation. Several Malay interviews required an interpreter working alongside the interviewer. The same interpreter then did the transcription and translation into English. All participants provided informed consent and their names have been replaced by pseudonyms in the following discussion to conceal their identities. The study procedure was approved by the university's Institutional Review Board. Following the fieldwork, the transcripts were coded according to

TABLE 8.1
Profile of Study Participants

Sex	Male	20
	Female	2
Age	40–49	3
	50–59	13
	60–69	5
	70–79	1
Race	Chinese	7
	Malay	14
	Indian	1
Marital status	Single	2
	Married	11
	Divorced	6
	Widowed	3
Family outside Singapore	Yes	13
	No	9
Country of residence before pandemic	Malaysia	13
	Indonesia	9
Nationality	Singapore Citizen	21
	Singapore PR	1
Highest education	Primary and below	9
	Secondary	8
	Vocational/certificate	4
	Diploma	1
Work status	Employed	13
	Unemployed	5
	Not working, not looking	4
Experience of rough sleeping	Yes	11
	No	11

FINDINGS

"I don't have anything here": Reconfiguring family

There was a striking similarity across the participants' accounts of their family relationships. Through a variety of circumstances, many of them had become untethered from their families. They described estrangement from their partners and children following marital conflict and divorce. Several had completely lost touch with their children. Others had grown apart from their siblings after their parents' death or due to misunderstandings. The gradual distancing from family often led to what is best described as a process of drift, when they left their family or matrimonial home and slipped into transient housing arrangements like sleeping at the workplace, staying with friends and sleeping rough. In Singapore, where public housing sold to married couples is the dominant housing option, moving away from family may imply the loss of social support and stable housing at the same time for lower-income persons, if they cannot afford to purchase housing again or encounter barriers in the social housing system (see later sections).

Grief from the death of a spouse or parent, or the end of a marriage, could even trigger a truncation of participants' lives in Singapore, a long period of overseas travel and, in some cases, relocation to another country. This sequence of life events emerged across several participants' accounts:

> Participant: I've been out of Singapore for the past three years. After my wife passed away, my mind is down, everything is down, I can't do anything much. This was quite...very long, drastic. I decided to give away all, everything, about Singapore. (Johan, male, 58 years old)

> Participant: I left Singapore because...you know, I'll be honest with you, whether you believe me or not. When you lost...you're the only son that look after her, when you lost her, you can't concentrate on work. About four months [later], I got a job in Jakarta and I go off. All my stuff, I given to my relative.

Interviewer: Did being away help? Being away in a different country?

Participant: Honestly, I do not want to see that house. Now if I go back to [that neighbourhood], I start to cry, you know? Because I remember like she's walking around there. She's been there for so many years. (Rehan, male, 54 years old)

Participant: That time, I was depressed. I stay there [in Malaysia], is because I don't want to have so much pressure, I want to throw all the… You know when you are sad, you want to throw all the past out? You, you do not want to see Singapore. When you want to change… you want to start your life new. (Keat, male, 51 years old)

As Mostowska (2013) observed, "the process of disaffiliation and isolation may either be a reason for leaving the country in the first place, or may be a consequence of migration" (p. 1132). For instance, after Keong (61 years old) left his parents' home in his early 30s, he had no housing and had to sleep in the taxi or bus that he was driving at the time. He later moved to Thailand where he lived for ten years in various transient housing arrangements. This was followed by 20 years in Malaysia, where he worked and slept in a coffeeshop. Being away eroded social connections in Singapore and made it difficult to find a trustworthy co-tenant to share the rent even if he were to move back:

I haven't come back to Singapore for so many years, the people I know are long gone. In the past, when I knew them, there were no handphones, only pagers. Not like now, only takes a phone call, where are you, let's have tea, you can WhatsApp. No such thing last time! We had to rely on the house phone and pager. We lost touch ever since I left… Some have moved… There's no way to find them.

Drift and disaffiliation did not always involve a complete dismantling of relationships. Even where there was conflict, family ties were sometimes reconfigured—even fondly cherished—rather than severed. During the interviews, without prompting, several participants showed the researchers photographs of loved ones folded away in their wallets or in their phones. Some received occasional telephone calls or visited family members when they were sick. Siblings sent food to the shelter during festive seasons and allowed their postal addresses to be used to receive mail. One participant said he could shower and get his laundry done at his sister's home when he was sleeping rough. Yet there were well-defined, if unspoken, boundaries. As Rahim (male, 68 years old) explained, when it came to communicating with his sons, "Very important ah, talk to him lah. No important, I cannot tell." Crucially, family members often drew the line at providing accommodation. When asked why they did not stay with family members who were supportive in other ways, almost all the participants said they did not want to "disturb" or "bother" their siblings or grown-up children, who had their own lives and families now. Some had been rejected or made to feel unwelcome in the past.

Moving to Malaysia or Indonesia offered participants the prospect of starting a new family in a new place. Some of them seemed to have adapted to their adoptive countries. They had lived there for many years and raised children with their Malaysian or Indonesian partners. They talked about finding jobs through friends and relatives helping to take care of their children. But others sounded less secure and settled. Livelihood was still a common concern. As Keat put it, "Do you think I want to go and stay there? No choice...the living standard in Singapore is too high." When asked about future plans, responses were mixed. Participants who were not married were most likely to contemplate resettling in Singapore after the pandemic, having been compelled by circumstances to stay for much longer than they anticipated. Among married participants with family overseas, some hoped to relocate to Singapore with their family, given the opportunity and resources. Others preferred to make a clean break and leave Singapore for good after the pandemic. In many instances, people had only vague and tentative plans that seemed consistent with the mobility and flux in their lives.

"I must find the money": Mobility and economic insecurity

Whereas disruptions and reconstructions of family ties form the backdrop to participants' transnational living arrangements, economic needs shape their decisions about where to live and the specific patterns of their mobility. Consistently, participants found living expenses in Singapore unaffordable, with housing (including rental) and food costs frequently cited as examples. Although a few participants faced pressures from debt and having to pay maintenance after divorce, the problem of expenses mainly reflected their low incomes. Due to Singapore's stronger currency, living in Malaysia or Indonesia was a form of arbitrage—a way to stretch their earnings and savings, as Keat explained in detail. Their migration decisions were extremely sensitive to costs, even outside of Singapore. Participants were knowledgeable about the differences in living costs between Malaysia and Indonesia, and between Batam and smaller towns in Indonesia. Some of them had moved between Malaysia, Indonesia and Thailand over the years. Still, low incomes continued to limit their housing options. Even outside Singapore, they usually rented rather than bought housing.

> Over there [in Malaysia], I rented a room, a nice room, it's only ringgit 650. So Singapore is only 200 plus. Singapore, you going to stay in a rental flat, it's very dear. 700, 800 Sing dollar, then I don't earn much, how to afford? Cannot, cannot afford. In Singapore, you want to spend every cent, you have to think. Over there, because of our money exchange, 1 to 3, so you know, you want to go to market, you want to buy what fish, you can go. Singapore, you have to consider. At least you live in more…freedom. No pressure. Singapore, every day you wake up, it's money. (Keat)

In terms of mobility patterns, there are two distinct groups: one that worked in Singapore but mostly lived in Malaysia or Indonesia, and another that both lived and worked in Malaysia or Indonesia. Both groups faced the risks and rigours of frequent border crossings. Neither fits the picture of a professional expatriate class or retirees seeking more comfortable facilities as described in the literature.

The first and more common scenario was to work in Singapore. These participants had long histories of employment in low-wage occupations like security officer, cleaner, food stall assistant, coffeeshop waiter, factory worker, construction worker, deckhand, supermarket assistant, hotel doorman, golf caddy, administrative assistant, sales promoter, printer technician and driver (i.e., bus, taxi, forklift, delivery truck, valet and private-hire car). They were usually casual or on-call workers, and rarely had assured hours or fixed incomes. If they were hired on contracts, these lasted anywhere from a few months to two years, often with breaks in between contracts when there was no income at all. At the time of the interviews, many had lost their jobs due to the pandemic. A few entered the pandemic unemployed as their contracts had ended or they had to stop work due to poor health. They lived on monthly payments from their Central Provident Fund (CPF) accounts[1] or short-term public financial assistance of several hundred dollars.

These participants had a similar social profile. They tended to be married, with their spouse and children living in Malaysia or Indonesia. Working in Singapore was seen as the best way to support their family as they were not formally allowed to work in Malaysia and Indonesia due to their visa status; besides, the wages would be "too small" in these countries. But this meant that they had to commute long distances. There were variations in travel patterns. Many commuted daily and recounted the fatigue, tight schedules and frustrations of getting caught in peak-hour traffic. One participant explained that if he was held up at work and missed the last ferry to Batam, he would have no shelter for the night. A few participants returned to their families once a week or saved up money and leave to visit once every few months. On their tight finances, they usually did not spend money on housing while in Singapore. Instead, they slept rough or at their workplaces. Such housing arrangements had often lasted for years.

The gap in living standards between Singapore and neighbouring countries reinforced the patriarchal structure of "mobile masculinity and localized femininity" long recognized in the migration literature (Amster and Lindquist 2005; Ong 1999, p. 20), and shaped the financial dynamic within these transnational families. Male participants saw themselves as the primary breadwinner in the marriage because they were Singaporean (men). Even when work was suspended during the lockdown, income had stopped and they were living on free meals at the shelter, none of them considered asking their spouses for money. As Awang (male, 68 years old) explained:

> Interviewer: So, your situation in the shelter, [your family in Indonesia] all know lah?
>
> Participant: They know, because when I stay here, I take photo, I show them [laughs].
>
> Interviewer: Oh okay. And they ever help you with anything?
>
> Participant: No lah, because the other side also very hard, right? We are Singapore, so we are the one...I the one who support there lah. No matter how, I must find the money. I must work.

In the second, less common arrangement, participants both lived and worked in Malaysia or Indonesia. In the past, many of them would have attempted but failed to find work in Singapore that paid adequately. After moving to Malaysia or Indonesia, they got by on very low incomes from informal work, for example, as a coffeeshop assistant or running a roadside food stall. In practical terms, this was just manageable because they were single, divorced or widowed, and did not have to support a family. As their visas were only valid for 30 days each time, they had to make a trip to Singapore and re-enter Malaysia or Indonesia every month. This was a regular but not uneventful routine in their lives (see next section). Each trip typically lasted only a few hours. Some participants also took the chance to visit relatives, attend medical appointments or do banking. When they had to stay overnight in Singapore, they slept rough.

"As long as our family is living together": Negotiating institutions

The most obvious institutional barrier the participants encountered was the tightened border regime and heightened surveillance of public spaces in response to COVID-19. They were not equally informed or prepared when the borders closed. Many were caught by surprise and came to Singapore with only a small backpack, thinking it would be another routine commute for work. A few managed to organize a hasty trip to Malaysia to gather some belongings and bid farewell to family before entering Singapore. No one expected that they would still be separated from their family many months later.

Once they reached the Singapore border, there was a process to identify and assist returning citizens who had no housing, so they could comply with rules to stay indoors. The wide range of experiences among the participants suggests there were inconsistencies in the process as the public health crisis rapidly evolved. For many participants, their shelter at the point of the interview was the third one they had been sent to within a few months, as certain facilities were redesignated for other purposes and new shelters became available. One participant somehow managed to slip through and slept rough outside a train station for a week before he was picked up by the police. Another person was particularly aggrieved because he had to use up all the cash he had on him to pay for a hotel stay before he was finally admitted to a shelter.

Even for a group so used to the rhythms of transnational living and makeshift housing arrangements, the pandemic threw their lives into disarray. The disruptions were so severe because of the brittleness of this pattern of living and participants' lack of resources. Being locked down in Singapore meant that they could not return to their families in Malaysia or Indonesia. Those who used to sleep rough while in Singapore could no longer do so. Job loss was also a loss of shelter for participants who had slept at their workplaces. Many participants spoke of their wish to return to their families soon, but knew they could not even if non-nationals were allowed into Malaysia and Indonesia, because they would not be able to afford testing and quarantine expenses, and delays to travel caused by quarantine requirements would cost them their jobs. It was striking that even in the extraordinary circumstances of the pandemic, participants still did not feel they could turn to their family in Singapore for help. The only remaining alternative to a shelter—staying at a hotel—was unaffordable.

The participants' problems with travel and housing during the lockdown were not a one-off, but an extension of the long-term insecurity borne of the basic contradiction that they were living permanently in places where they only had short-stay rights (i.e., Malaysia or Indonesia), yet could only make brief visits to the country where they had permanent citizenship rights (i.e., Singapore).

Transnational living necessitated frequent border crossings and repeated encounters with immigration laws and border institutions (Oh and Jagtiani 2016). As social visit pass holders in Malaysia or Indonesia, they were only allowed to stay for up to 30 days each time. They had to exit then re-enter these countries every month to "chop passport" (i.e., get their passports stamped and visas renewed). Their crowded passports regularly drew attention from immigration officers. Participants had learnt strategies to deal with this, such as timing their arrival at the immigration checkpoint during less busy hours when officers were more amenable to persuasion. These encounters were described in a matter-of-fact way, as something beyond their control and which they had come to accept. There was an understanding that their living arrangements—using a social visit pass for what is essentially long-term residence—lay in a grey area within immigration rules.

As social visit pass holders, participants did not enjoy the same rights as citizens. They had no legal right to work, so were limited to informal employment in low-paying odd jobs. Participants clearly felt self-conscious about this. Those who spoke about it took a while to open up, initially describing their work as "helping out a friend" or "doing charity work". They also faced strict rules on homeownership.

If they bought housing, it had to be in their spouses' name, since the spouses were nationals. These practices are reminiscent of Khamsya's (2016) accounts of older Singaporeans living illegally in low-cost housing meant for Malaysians, who sought to lower their visibility and avoid contact with formal institutions. These constraints also affected economic and housing security. In the most striking case, Keong lived in Malaysia for 20 years but, in his words, "never had a home".

Many participants had experienced a different set of housing challenges in Singapore before they moved overseas. Singapore's public housing policies perform multiple roles. Apart from addressing housing needs, they are also powerful tools for social regulation and encouraging asset-building (Ng 2020). To promote the heteronormative nuclear family, complex rules of eligibility and priority differentiate between people by marital status. The public housing system is further bifurcated along the lines of property ownership. Owner-occupation is encouraged and incentivized, whereas a highly residualized social rental sector representing just five to six per cent of the public housing stock is of poor quality and subject to strict gatekeeping.

For the male participants, the matrimonial flat was typically ceded to the ex-wife after divorce. As they also had limited savings or had to settle debts, they could not afford to purchase another flat. The only feasible option for many participants was therefore social renting. But here, they encountered other barriers. Those who had sold a flat were barred from social renting for 30 months. Participants with a Malaysian or Indonesian spouse were not eligible to access social housing as a couple (unless the spouse had Permanent Resident status in Singapore), ruling out living in Singapore as a family. Several participants had considered applying for social housing as singles. But if they did, they would be subject to the Joint Singles Scheme which requires them to share a small studio flat (measuring around 35 square metres, with no separate bedrooms) with another single co-tenant. The lack of space and privacy was not just a problem in terms of daily living, as described by Huat (male, 54 years old), it also meant that spouses would not be able to stay during visits to Singapore:

> I do not know why they want to put two total strangers together. I mean, I always ask the person a question, do you married? Would you marry a man or a woman you met less than five minutes, you say, hey let's move in together? Then this guy will want to move out, or they will start fighting each other. But this is HDB[2]!

These housing barriers within Singapore's public housing system on the one hand, and restrictions on homeownership in Malaysia and Indonesia on the other, contributed to participants' reliance on various temporary and insecure housing arrangements. A case that stood out was Tiong (52 years old), whose family of four lived apart because they could not afford housing for the entire family and his application for social housing was unsuccessful. He worked in Singapore but rented a place in Malaysia; his Malaysian wife lived in staff accommodation in Singapore; his older son had just completed military service in Singapore and was renting a single bedroom; his younger son was in military service and lived in army quarters. In his words, "our greatest wish is for us to be able to afford a house regardless of whether it is three-room flat, as long as our family is living together".

CONCLUSION

The interviews in this study reveal a distinct group of people who experience housing insecurity in connection with transnational living. Existing archetypes of Singaporeans migrating to Malaysia and Indonesia as a lifestyle choice clearly do not fit. Instead, for this group, their transition to transnational living follows a series of life events involving their social, economic and institutional dislocation, which also pushes them into precarious housing arrangements. As Ong (1999) observes, "travelling subjects are never free of regulations set by state power, market operations and kinship norms" (p. 19). While their mobility may be a survival strategy and response to initial hardship, it nevertheless places them in a state of "dual liminality" where housing security is still unobtainable (Oh and Jagtiani 2016, p. 274). In contrast to forms of transnational householding where migrants continue to contribute resources towards the upkeep of their family in their country of origin, these migrants have only weak ties with their family in Singapore and do not have a base to which they may return in a crisis. But neither are they fully engaged in the kind of long-term social capital projects that Khamsya (2016) describes on the other side. Rather, their lives are characterized by varying degrees of uncertainty, impermanence and anxiety as they continue to negotiate family obligations, economic challenges, and policy barriers.

Research on the reasons for homelessness in Singapore as well as in other societies, point to the interaction of structural and individual factors within the context of individual life trajectories. These include poverty, unemployment, insecure work, barriers to housing and other services, relationship breakdown, family violence, health problems, incarceration and substance use (Anderson 2004; Batterham 2019; Broll and Huey 2020; Jasni et al. 2020; Somerville 2013). This account is also largely accurate of transnational persons who experience housing insecurity, except for two additional distinguishing features. The first is that circumstances following a process of social disaffiliation lead to an opportunity to move to another country, perhaps because of advice from friends or a relationship with a national of that country. The second is that entering a transnational living arrangement sets in motion a pattern of mobility that itself generates risks of housing insecurity, via encounters with border, migration and housing regimes. The inherent risks of stranding in carefully coordinated and high-frequency border crossings also set apart the housing insecurity of mobile transnationals from the housing barriers faced by migrants seeking permanent relocation.

When comparing the accounts of participants who had and had not slept rough, there were far more similarities than differences. Among married participants, those who crossed the border and returned to their families at the end of each workday were less likely to sleep rough, while those who stayed in Singapore for weeks or months at a time were more likely to report episodes of rough sleeping because they had no reliable housing arrangements in Singapore. Among unmarried participants, those not working in Singapore usually did not need to sleep rough. Only a few reported having slept in public places when they were facing serious financial problems. Except for these, the participants were similar in their lack of social and economic resources, and their problems with housing and migration policies. These are the commonalities that pushed them into homelessness when the borders closed. The findings suggest that while street homelessness, as the severest form of housing deprivation, will always be of interest to city planners and service providers, persistent and underlying housing insecurity may be more fruitful areas of research and must be the long-term target of policy intervention.

Collectively, these individual narratives suggest new angles for interpreting a global city like Singapore. A longstanding image of the global city is that it draws human capital from other places, both professionals with specialized skills and low-wage migrants from less developed economies (Sassen 2002; Yeoh and Chang 2001). In Singapore, where migrants are a critical element of a finely calibrated national economic strategy, chosen and deployed according to a hierarchy of value, it is jarring to discover an outflow of citizens who are displaced by economic competition and move down the income gradient to societies that are less competitive but more hospitable. Some of the difficulties they face in their new host societies, such as in housing, evoke the restrictions imposed on foreign nationals categorized as low-skilled workers in Singapore. The contingent nature of their mobility and their capacity to adapt and find opportunity are a useful reminder that state visions and strategies—even in places with strong central command and control—do not fully anticipate and account for migration experiences.

For any study conducted during an extraordinary event like the COVID-19 pandemic, the question of generalisability will arise. Clearly, participants entered the shelter due to the pandemic and related public health measures. Some of them had lost employment because of it. But for the most part, the social context, economic circumstances and institutional barriers related to their mobility and housing insecurity were present long before. Their issues became more severe and observable during the pandemic—presenting a rare opportunity for a study like this—but were not primarily caused by it. For Singapore specifically, the most pressing problems are low wages, inadequate social protection and gaps in the social housing system. These conditions do not only affect housing security directly—they also weigh on decisions to enter a transnational living arrangement that may then introduce additional housing challenges. Policy responses to these challenges will determine whether the participants and others like them have genuine prospects of securing adequate housing for themselves and their families.

NOTES

Acknowledgement: The authors are grateful to the study participants, the social workers who facilitated recruitment and Terence Teo who helped to conduct interviews.

1. These are mandatory individual savings accounts, made up of employer and employee contributions, mainly for retirement, housing and health purposes.

2. Housing Development Board, the public housing authority in Singapore

REFERENCES

Acting Director General of Immigration. 2020. "Temporary Prohibitions of Entry (Travel Ban) into Indonesia for Foreigners in Response to COVID-19's Outbreak". Embassy of the Republic of Indonesia in Manila, the Republic of the Philippines, 31 March 2020. https://kemlu.go.id/manila/en/read/temporary-prohibitions-of-entry-travel-ban-into-indonesia-for-foreigners-in-response-to-covid-19s-outbreak/1003/important-information.

Amster, Matthew H. and Johan Lindquist. 2005. "Frontiers, Sovereignty and Marital Tactics: Comparisons from the Borneo Highlands and the Indonesia-Malaysia-Singapore Growth Triangle". *The Asia Pacific Journal of Anthropology* 6, no. 1: 1–17.

Amundson, Erik. 2017. "European Transnational Migration and Homelessness in Scandinavia". *International Journal of Migration, Health and Social Care* 13, no. 1: 26–38.

Anderson, Isobel. 2004. "Housing, Homelessness and the Welfare State in the UK". *European Journal of Housing Policy* 4, no. 3: 369–89.

Barbu, Simona, Sergio P. Barranco, and Ruby Silk. 2021. "The Impact of COVID-19 on Homeless Service Providers and Homeless People". *Cityscape* 23, no. 2: 361–80.

Batterham, Deb. 2019. "Defining 'At-risk of Homelessness': Re-connecting Causes, Mechanisms and Risk". *Housing, Theory and Society* 36, no. 1: 1–24.

Beaverstock, Jonathan V. 2002. "Transnational Elites in Global Cities: British Expatriates in Singapore's Financial District". *Geoforum* 33: 525–38.

Benavides, Abraham D. and Julius A. Nukpezah. 2020. "How Local Governments are Caring for the Homeless during the COVID-19 Pandemic". *American Review of Public Administration* 50, nos. 6–7: 650–57.

Benfer, Emily A., David Vlahov, Marissa Y. Long, Evan Walker-Wells, Pottenger Jr., Gregg Gonsalves, and Danya E. Keene. 2021. "Eviction, Health Inequity and the Spread of COVID-19: Housing Policy as a Primary Pandemic Mitigation Strategy". *Journal of Urban Health* 98: 1–12.

Broll, Ryan and Laura Huey. 2020. "'Every Time I Try to Get Out, I Get Pushed Back': The Role of Violent Victimisation in Women's Experience of Multiple Episodes of Homelessness". *Journal of Interpersonal Violence* 35, nos. 17–18: 3379–3404.

Busch-Geertsema, Volker, Dennis Culhane, and Suzanne Fitzpatrick. 2015. *A Global Framework for Understanding and Measuring Homelessness*. Chicago: Institute of Global Homelessness.

Campbell, Howard and Josué G. Lachica. 2013. "Transnational Homelessness: Finding a Place on the US–Mexico Border". *Journal of Borderlands Studies* 28, no. 3: 279–90. https://doi.org/10.1080/08865655.2013.863441.

Chia, Osmond. 2021. "S'pore Man with No Place to Stay after Return from Batam Gets 7 Weeks' Jail for Working during SHN". *Straits Times*, 2 December 2021. https://www.straitstimes.com/singapore/courts-crime/homeless-man-in-spore-jailed-7-weeks-for-working-during-covid-19-stay-home.

CNA. 2018. "Clearing the Causeway: Johor Pledges Smoother Journey by Any Means Necessary". CNA, 9 June 2018. https://www.channelnewsasia.com/asia/causeway-johor-bahru-commute-second-link-816491. https://infographics.channelnewsasia.com/interactive/causewayjam/index.html.

———. 2020. "Malaysia Bars Citizens from Going Overseas, Foreigners from Entering Country for 2 Weeks to Curb COVID-19 Spread: PM Muhyiddin". CNA, 16 March 2020. https://www.channelnewsasia.com/asia/malaysia-bars-citizens-overseas-foreigners-entering-covid19-772361.

Crisis. 2021. *Home for All: Why EU Citizens are More Likely to Experience Homelessness – and Why It Matters*. London: Crisis.

Daly, Gerald. 1996. "Migrants and Gate Keepers: The Links between Immigration and Homelessness in Western Europe". *Cities* 13, no. 1: 11–23.

Directorate General of Immigration. 2020. "Temporary Entry Restrictions to Indonesia During COVID-19 Outbreak". Japanese Embassy in Indonesia, 4 April 2020. https://www.id.emb-japan.go.jp/nyuukan_eng.pdf.

Djuve, Anne B., Jon H. Friberg, Guri Tyldum, and Huafeng Zhang. 2015. *When Poverty Meets Affluence: Migrants from Romania on the Streets of the Scandinavian Capitals*. Oslo; Copenhagen: Fafo; The Rockwool Foundation.

Fitzpatrick, Suzanne, Beth Watts, and Rhiannon Sims. 2020. *Homelessness Monitor England 2020: COVID-19 Crisis Response Briefing*. London: Crisis.

Fitzpatrick, Suzanne, Glen Bramley, Janice Blenkinsopp, Sarah Johnsen, Mandy Littlewood, Gina Netto, Filip Sosenko, and Beth Watts. 2015. *Destitution in the UK: An Interim Report*. York: Joseph Rowntree Foundation.

Goh, Daniel P.S. 2019. "Super-diversity and the Bio-politics of Migrant Worker Exclusion in Singapore". *Identities* 26, no. 3: 356–73. https://doi.org/10.1080/1070289X.2018.1530899.

Goh, Yan Han. 2020. "Sufficient Safe Shelter Capacity for the Homeless during Circuit Breaker: Desmond Lee". *Straits Times*, 24 April 2020. https://www.straitstimes.com/singapore/sufficient-safe-shelter-capacity-for-the-homeless-duringcircuit-breaker-desmond-lee.

Harris, Ebrahim and Joseph Campbell. 2021. "For Stranded Father, Bittersweet Reunion as Singapore-Malaysia Border Reopens". Reuters, 2 December 2021. https://www.reuters.com/world/asia-pacific/stranded-father-bittersweet-reunion-singapore-malaysia-border-reopens-2021-12-01/.

Ho, Yi-Jian and Adam D. Tyson. 2011. "Malaysian Migration to Singapore: Pathways, Mechanisms and Status". *Malaysian Journal of Economic Studies* 48, no. 2: 131–45.

Hof, Helena. 2019. "The Eurostars Go Global: Young Europeans' Migration to Asia for Distinction and Alternative Life Paths". *Mobilities* 14, no. 6: 923–39. https://doi.org/10.1080/17450101.2019.1643164.

Honorato, Bruno E. and Ana C. Oliveira. 2020. "Homeless Population and COVID-19". *Brazilian Journal of Public Administration* 54, no. 4: 1064–78.

Järv, Olle, Ago Tominga, Kerli Müürisepp, and Siiri Silm. 2021. "The Impact of COVID-19 on Daily Lives of Transnational People based on Smartphone Data: Estonians in Finland". *Journal of Location Based Services* 15, no. 3: 169–97. https://doi.org/10.1080/17489725.2021.1887526.

Jasni, Mohd Alif Bin, Siti Hajar Abu Bakar Ah, and Norruzeyati Che Mohd Nasir. 2020. "Three Major Interrelated Factors Contributing to Homelessness Issue among Former Prisoners in Malaysia". *International Journal of Criminology and Sociology* 9: 415–30.

Kaur, Amarjit. 2006. "Order (and Disorder) at the Borders: Mobility, International Labour Migration and Border Controls in Southeast Asia". In *Mobility, Labor Migration and Border Controls in Asia*, edited by Amarjit Kaur and Ian Metcalfe, pp. 23–51. Hampshire, UK: Palgrave Macmillan.

Kelleher, Joanne and Michelle Norris. 2020. *Day Services for People who are Homeless in Dublin: A Review Commissioned by the Dublin Region Homeless Executive*. Dublin: Dublin Region Homeless Executive.

Khamsya, Bin Khidzer Mohammad. 2016. "'Balik Kampung': The Practice of Transborder Retirement Migration in Johor, Malaysia". In *International Migration in Southeast Asia: Continuities and Discontinuities*, edited by Kwen Fee Lian, Md Mizanur Rahman and Yabit bin Alas, pp. 57–82. Singapore: Springer.

Lam, Theodora, Brenda S.A. Yeoh, and Lisa Law. 2002. "Sustaining Families Transnationally: Chinese-Malaysians in Singapore". *Asia and Pacific Migration Journal* 11, no. 1: 117–43.

Lian, Kwen Fee, Md Mizanur Rahman and Yabit bin Alas. 2016. "Making Sense of Inter and Intraregional Mobility in Southeast Asia". In *International Migration in Southeast Asia: Continuities and Discontinuities*, edited by Kwen Fee Lian, Md Mizanur Rahman and Yabit bin Alas. Singapore: Springer.

Liu, Vanessa. 2020. "Call for More Help as Shelters for the Homeless Hit Full Capacity During Covid-19 Circuit Breaker Period". *Straits Times*, 18 April 2020. https://www.straitstimes.com/singapore/call-for-more-help-as-shelters-for-the-homeless-hit-full-capacity.

Meah, Natasha. 2021. "The Big Read: After More than 500 days, Home Remains a Bridge too far for Malaysians stuck in Singapore". CNA, 9 August 2021.

https://www.channelnewsasia.com/singapore/malaysians-workers-stuck-singapore-2098701.
Ministry of Health. 2020a. "Additional Measures for Travellers to Reduce Further Importation of COVID-19 Cases", 18 March 2020. https://www.moh.gov.sg/news-highlights/details/additional-measures-for-travellers-to-reduce-further-importation-of-covid-19-cases.
———. 2020b. "Additional Border Control Measures to Reduce Further Importation of COVID-19 Cases", 22 March 2020. https://www.moh.gov.sg/news-highlights/details/additional-border-control-measures-to-reduce-further-importation-of-covid-19-cases.
———. 2020c. "Tighter Measures to Minimise Further Spread of COVID-19", 24 March 2020. https://www.moh.gov.sg/news-highlights/details/tighter-measures-to-minimise-further-spread-of-covid-19.
Montsion, Jean Michel. 2012. "When Talent Meets Mobility: Un/desirability in Singapore's New Citizenship Project". *Citizenship Studies* 16, nos. 3–4: 469–82. https://doi.org/10.1080/13621025.2012.683259.
Mostowska, Magdalena. 2013. "Migration and Homelessness: The Social Networks of Homeless Poles in Oslo". *Journal of Ethnic and Migration Studies* 39, no. 7: 1125–40. https://doi.org/10.1080/1369183X.2013.778037.
Ng, Kok-Hoe. 2019. *Homeless in Singapore: Results from a Nationwide Street Count*. Singapore: Lee Kuan Yew School of Public Policy, National University of Singapore.
———. 2020. "Social Housing". In *Housing Practice Series: Singapore*, pp. 10–27. Nairobi: UN Habitat.
Ng, Kok-Hoe and Jeyda Simren Sekhon Atac. 2022. *Seeking Shelter: Homeless during the COVID-19 Pandemic in Singapore*. Singapore: Lee Kuan Yew School of Public Policy, National University of Singapore.
OECD. 2021. HC3.2. *National Strategies for Combating Homelessness*. Paris: OECD Directorate of Employment, Labour and Social Affairs.
Oh, Su-Ann and Reema B. Jagtiani. 2016. "Singaporeans Living in Johor and Batam: Next-door Transnationalism Living and Border Anxiety". In *The SIJORI Cross-border Region: Transnational Politics, Economics and Culture*, edited by Francis E. Hutchinson and Terence Chong, pp. 267–92. Singapore: ISEAS – Yusof Ishak Institute.
Ong, Aihwa. 1999. *Flexible Citizenship: The Cultural Logics of Transnationality*. Durham and London: Duke University Press.
Ormond, Meghann. 2014. "Resorting to Plan J: Population Perceptions of Singaporean Retirement Migration to Johor, Malaysia". *Asian and Pacific Migration Journal* 23, no. 1: 1–26.
Parliament of Victoria. 2021. *Inquiry into Homelessness in Victoria: Final Report*. Victoria: Victorian Government Printer.

Parsell, Cameron, Andrew Clarke, and Ella Kuskoff. 2020. "Understanding Responses to Homelessness during COVID-19: An Examination of Australia". *Housing Studies*. https://doi.org/10.1080/02673037.2020.1829564.

Pleace, Nicholas. 2010. "Immigration and Homelessness". In *Homelessness Research in Europe*, edited by Eoino O'Sullivan, Volker Busch-Geertsema, Deborah Quilgars and Nicholas Pleace. Brussels: FEANTSA.

Rahman, Serina. 2021. "Borderland without Business: The Economic Impact of Covid-19 on Peninsular Malaysia's Southernmost State of Johor". *ISEAS Perspective*, no. 2021/65, 7 May 2021. https://www.iseas.edu.sg/articles-commentaries/iseas-perspective/2021-65-borderland-without-business-the-economic-impact-of-covid-19-on-peninsular-malaysias-southernmost-state-of-johor-by-serina-rahman/.

Rizzo, Agatino and John Glasson. 2011. "Conceiving Transit Space in Singapore/Johor: A Research Agenda for the Strait Transnational Urban Region (STUR)". *International Journal of Urban Sustainable Development* 3, no. 2: 156–67.

Sassen, Saskia. 2002. *The Global City: New York, London, Tokyo*. Princeton, NJ: Princeton University Press.

Shahare, Virendra B. 2021. "COVID-19 Lockdown: The Neglected Migrant Workers in India". *Asia Pacific Journal of Social Work and Development* 31, nos. 1–2: 97–104. https://doi.org/10.1080/02185385.2021.1875335.

Smith, Lucy. 2018. *Mind the Gap: Homelessness Amongst Newly Recognised Refugees*. Newcastle Upon Tyne: NACCOM.

―――. 2019. *Mind the Gap One Year on: Continuation Report on Homelessness Amongst Newly Recognised Refugees*. Newcastle Upon Tyne: NACCOM.

Somerville, Peter. 2013. "Understanding Homelessness". *Housing, Theory and Society* 30, no. 4: 384–415.

Spyratou, Dominika. 2020. "How COVID-19 Has Highlighted the Anti-migration Agenda in Greece". In *Homeless in Europe: The Impact of COVID-19 on Homeless People and Services*. Brussels: FEANTSA.

Tai, Janice and Toh Yong Chuan. 2015. "Singaporeans Pack JB Nursing Homes". *Straits Times*, 16 March 2015. https://www.asiaone.com/singaporeans-pack-jb-nursing-homes.

Tai, Po-Fen. 2006. "Social Polarisation: Comparing Singapore, Hong Kong and Taipei". *Urban Studies* 43, no. 10: 1737–56.

Testaverde, Mauro, Harry Moroz, Claire H. Hollweg, and Achim Schmillen. 2017. *Migrating to Opportunity: Overcoming Barriers to Labor Mobility in Southeast Asia*. Washington, D.C.: World Bank.

Toyota, Mika and Biao Xiang. 2012. "The Emerging Transnational 'Retirement Industry' in Southeast Asia". *International Journal of Sociology and Social Policy* 32, no. 11/12: 708–19.

Udechukwu, Treasure, Lorraine Harnett, Mzwandile A. Mabhala, and John Reid. 2021. *COVID-19 and People Experiencing Homelessness: Reported Measures Implemented in the European Region during the Pandemic*. Brussels: The Association of Schools of Public Health in the European Region (ASPHER).

Wang, Ying, Lei Hua, Shuyun Zou, Taofeng Deng, Yongqi Chen, Wanying Cao, Chuhan Wu, Yujie Zhou, and Hua Zou. 2021. "The Homeless People in China during the COVID-19 Pandemic: Victims of the Strict Pandemic Control Measures of the Government". *Frontiers in Public Health* 9: 1–16.

Wilczek, Jakub. 2020. "How has the Coronavirus Outbreak Affected the Homeless Shelter System in Poland?" In *Homeless in Europe: The Impact of COVID-19 on Homeless People and Services*. Brussels: FEANTSA.

Ye, Junjia and Philip F. Kelly. 2011. "Cosmopolitanism at Work: Labour Market Exclusion in Singapore's Financial Sector". *Journal of Ethnic and Migration Studies* 37, no. 5: 691–707. https://doi.org/10.1080/1369183X.2011.559713.

Yeoh, Brenda S.A. 2006. "Bifurcated Labour: The Unequal Incorporation of Transmigrants in Singapore". *Tijdschrift voor Economische en Sociale Geografie* 97, no. 1: 26–37.

Yeoh, Brenda S.A., Grace Baey, Maria Platt, and Kellynn Wee. 2017. "Bangladeshi Construction Workers and the Politics of (Im)mobility in Singapore". *City* 21, no. 5: 641–49. https://doi.org/10.1080/13604813.2017.1374786.

Yeoh, Brenda S.A. and T.C. Chang. 2001. "Globalising Singapore: Debating Transnational Flows in the City". *Urban Studies* 3, no. 7: 1025–44.

Yusof, Zaihan Mohamed. 2020. "Coronavirus: Mad Rush for Malaysian Workers to go home to Johor Baru and then Return to S'pore". *Straits Times*, 17 March 2020. https://www.straitstimes.com/singapore/mad-rush-for-malaysian-workers-to-go-home-in-johor-baru-and-return-to-spore.

Zhan, Shaohua, Rajiv Aricat, and Min Zhou. 2020. "New Dynamics of Multinational Migration: Chinese and Indian Migrants in Singapore and Los Angeles". *Geographical Research* 58: 365–76.

9

OLDER PERSONS WITH HEARING DISABILITIES IN INDONESIA: VULNERABILITY AND DEMOGRAPHIC DIVERSITY DURING THE COVID-19 PANDEMIC

Evi Nurvidya Arifin, Chang-Yau Hoon and Aris Ananta

INTRODUCTION

The outbreak of COVID-19 in 2019 has affected the quality of life of individuals all over the world. The direct effects include being infected by the virus, whether asymptomatic, pre-symptomatic, or being severely ill and even loss their life. Family suffering, financial loss, and the inability of health facilities to accommodate the rapidly rising cases have aggravated the misery of those being exposed to the virus.

The indirect effects are experienced through various health protocols, including restrictions on population mobility and universal face masking to limit the spread of the virus. These indirect effects may influence people's livelihood, day-to-day behaviour, and mental health. The vulnerable groups (such as the poor, older persons, pregnant women, and persons with disabilities) may suffer much more, facing difficult choices between being exposed to the virus by continuing their usual daily activities or going hungry by staying at home and losing their income.

Among these vulnerable groups, older persons with a hearing disability may suffer more. Policies to curb the spread of infection bring difficulties in face-to-face communication for persons with hearing disabilities (Sher et al. 2020). The mask muddles sound and hides the movement of the lip (Trecca et al. 2020; Huzlen and Fabry 2020). Physical distancing also prevents people with hearing disabilities from communicating well with others as distance reduces the clarity of voice (Huzlen and Fabry 2020). Furthermore, restriction on meeting other persons physically results in having fewer opportunities to obtain assistance in daily conversation.

Therefore, older persons with hearing disabilities are much more precarious, vulnerable and marginalized than others during the COVID-19 pandemic. The challenges are accentuated in the absence of affordable effective hearing aids and limited or even non-existence of sign language.

Nevertheless, hearing disability during the pandemic is one of the most often neglected topics in research and policymaking, although the disability has far-reaching consequences on the quality of life (Nuesse et al. 2021), prosperity of the community, and government policies (WHO 2021; McDaida et al. 2021). This study examines the magnitude and prevalence of hearing disability among older persons, their demographic diversity and hearing disability impacts on the quality of life. This knowledge will be helpful for older persons to improve their quality of life and empowers them to contribute economically and socially to society during the pandemic. These findings are important inputs and lessons for policymakers to design policies to reduce the precarity of older persons' wellbeing, especially during the COVID-19 pandemic.

Through its national statistical office (Badan Pusat Statistik), the Indonesian government has collected data on hearing disabilities. However, the data have not been analysed sufficiently. Therefore, there has not been any comprehensive statistical study on hearing disability among older persons in Indonesia. This chapter fills this research gap. It conducts a statistical study on hearing disability in Indonesia, the most populous Southeast Asian country, which has around 270 million people and is experiencing rapid population ageing. This chapter aims to produce the first statistics and comprehensive statistical analysis of the magnitude and prevalence of hearing disability among older persons at the national and provincial levels.

This chapter delves into the demographic diversity of the prevalence. It examines the association between hearing disability and quality of life, indicated by employment, health status, communication and psychological wellbeing and the use of digital technology. Finally, it provides policy recommendations on how to minimize the capability deprivation resulting from hearing disability. These can be lessons for policy designs during a pandemic such as the COVID-19.

The statistical analysis is based on the raw data of the 2018 National Social and Economic Survey (SUSENAS). The survey was conducted two years prior to the pandemic outbreak in Indonesia in March 2020. As hearing disability is likely to be irreversible, the pattern from the 2018 data remains relevant to the situation during the pandemic. The data is expected to shed light on the challenges that older persons with hearing disability face during the COVID-19 pandemic.

HEARING DISABILITY AS CAPABILITY DEPRIVATION

The capability approach focuses on individuals' freedom to do and to be. Expansion of individual freedom is both an end and a goal of development. Therefore, attention must be focused on how to expand this freedom, and provide more choices for the individuals to do and to be (Sen 2009). Capabilities refer to practical opportunities, given the available choices. They are not observable. It is different from functioning, which is a "fact", and the actual performance of what the individuals want to do or to be.

An illustration is the use of a hearing aid among people with hearing disabilities. Without the aid, an individual has limited opportunities to listen, participate and communicate in daily life. The hearing aid has therefore minimized the individual's hearing disability by allowing the individual to better listen, participate and communicate in society.

This approach provides a new paradigm in understanding disability, along with its socio-economic determinants and consequences. Disability is a critical factor of capability deprivation, limiting a person's freedom to do and to be in their everyday life. Persons with disability are among the most deprived members of society, and they are often much neglected. They and their families tend to live in poverty. Furthermore, life for them is more "costly" than the able-bodied people because they need more income to do the same things such as daily routine activities. Furthermore, due to limited choices and opportunities in employment, their disability may likely result in limited opportunities to earn income, and this may bring more severe disability (Sen 2009).[1]

One advantage of the capability deprivation approach is when we are dealing with irreversible cases such as hearing disability. The question is then how to minimize these hearing capability deprivations. Furthermore, effective public policies may also be made to prevent the onset of disabilities, delay the onset of disabilities and/or slow down the progression of the disabilities, although in certain cases, disabilities can be inherited. The answer to this question requires an understanding of the four sources of capability deprivation identified by Sen (2009), which can be used to address policies and programmes.

The first source of capability deprivation is demographic diversity such as age, sex, education, marital status, health (including disability), ethnicity/race, religion and language. Age is a clear example of one source of capability deprivation. The older the persons, the more likely they are to experience disabilities such as hearing disability.

The second is the physical environment where the persons live. Individuals may not be able to change the physical environment where they live, such as areas with high pollution index or prone to floods. A noisy place may worsen the inability to hear for people with hearing disabilities. Living in urban areas may expose persons to more noise and therefore worsen people hearing capability deprivation.

The third is the social infrastructure, such as the availability of public health services, affordable high-quality education, affordable high-quality internet services, accessible and affordable high-quality hearing aids, friendly public transportation to persons with hearing disabilities, and the absence of crime.

The fourth is relational perspectives or social norms, including how to be seen in public, maintain proper manner and follow community tradition. In many societies, wearing a hearing aid may create social stigma, such as harassment. Another example is workplace discrimination against persons with hearing disabilities, as co-workers may not be patient to communicate with persons having hearing disabilities. Employers' preference for able-bodied workers also deprives the opportunity for persons with hearing disabilities to work.

HEARING DISABILITY DURING THE PANDEMIC

Before the pandemic, people with hearing disabilities in developing countries, including Indonesia, often do not have adequate access to hearing aids, hearing tests, or treatment for hearing problems. Even if hearing aids are available, their price may be too high for people in the countries. Affordability of hearing aid has been one of the main issues in minimizing capability deprivation of persons with hearing disabilities, especially those with moderate or severe difficulty to hear.[2] As discussed in Alqudah et al. (2021), the pandemic increases their hearing capabilities deprivation, regardless of the degree of the disability—mild, moderate, or severe (including deaf).

The unintended consequence of using facial masks to prevent virus transmission through droplets is a reduction in the audibility of voice transmission from another person (Trecca et al. 2020). This deprives the capability of persons with hearing disabilities to comprehend conversations because they cannot read the lip movements of the people they are speaking.

The difficulty in understanding conversation depends on the type of facial mask being used. There are generally three types of facial masks worn during this pandemic: N95, medical or surgical masks, and non-medical facial masks. The use of facial masks reduces voice attenuation, especially the high-frequency voice. For instance, the surgical mask can reduce the voice attenuation by 2–3 decibels (dB), while the N95 by almost 12 dB in comparison to normal communication without a facial mask (Huzlen and Fabry 2020). Thus, the volume of one's voice becomes lower. A noisy background can further reduce the attenuation of voice or sound, making communication very difficult.

Furthermore, physical distancing makes one's voice difficult to hear among people with hearing disabilities. When social norms require the conversational distance to change from 1 metre to at least 1.5 metres, the speech audibility becomes less. It is not only the distance that matters but also the missing facial expression, which is part of effective communication.

Trecca et al. (2020) argued that hearing function decreases further when persons with hearing disabilities become sick and need to receive medical treatments in health facilities. Their findings from a small sample of respondents with mild and profound hearing disabilities showed that most of them had more difficulties in communicating with medical staff who wore personal protection equipment (PPE). Their ability to hear could worsen if they did not wear hearing aids.

Even with hearing aids, communication can be frustrating when both parties wear facial masks. In addition, Huzlen and Fabry (2020) have noted how environmental factors in hospitals can worsen patients' hearing capability deprivation. These factors included the lighting and noise caused by various medical equipment in the hospitals or clinics and the expected norms to lower the volume to respect the other patients' space.

Yet, some innovative ideas have emerged in Indonesia. A deaf Indonesian couple in Makassar[3] produces cloth facial masks with transparent plastic in the middle, enabling lip reading and viewing facial expressions. They produce these transparent masks, sell and share them with other people with hearing disabilities. However, these masks cannot be much of help if those without hearing disabilities do not use these masks. This phenomenon is also observed in other districts in Indonesia, such as Wonogiri[4] and Sleman.[5] This innovative mask not only helps them to communicate with other people having hearing disabilities but also has brought economic opportunity during the economic crisis caused by the COVID-19 pandemic.

DATA

The main data source for the cross-tabulation analysis in this chapter is the 2018 National Social and Economic Survey (SUSENAS). As mentioned earlier, this is pre-pandemic data, as the latest data was not available when this chapter was prepared. In addition, the prevalence of hearing disability may not change rapidly in a short period. Thus, we can expect that the 2018 data is still highly relevant to reflect the issues related to older persons with hearing disabilities during the COVID-19 pandemic.

SUSENAS is a nationally representative household survey covering all provinces collected by Badan Pusat Statistik (Statistics Indonesia). This survey is conducted twice a year (March and September) with different sample coverages. Our discussion for this chapter uses the larger March survey, covering about 300,000 households selected using probability sampling with a three-step sampling approach. Information was collected from all members of the selected households. The March 2018 questionnaire includes globally standardized questions on disabilities, such as those in the Washington Group on Disability Statistics (Groce and Mont 2017). This statistic includes disabilities in seeing, hearing, walking, hand gripping, concentrating, self-caring, communicating, and controlling emotion. Each is measured with a Likert Scale.

WHO ARE THE OLDER PERSONS IN INDONESIA IN 2018?

This chapter follows the Indonesian official definition of older persons as people aged 60 years and above. Their percentage doubled in almost half of the century, from 4.5 per cent in 1971 to 9.3 per cent in 2018. Indonesia was home to 24.9 million older persons in 2018, which is the largest number in Southeast Asia, scattered across 34 provinces. They are not a homogenous group. They have diverse backgrounds. The majority (63.4 per cent) of them were the "young old", 60–69 years old; 27.9 per cent were the "old", 70–79 years old, and 8.7 percent were the "oldest old" (80 years and above). As the young old made up more than half of the population, this group can be seen as untapped resources for development if their onset of disabilities can be delayed, the progress of disabilities can be slowed down, and capability deprivation can be minimized.

As in many other countries, older women outnumber older men as women generally outlive men. Life expectancy at birth for women and men was 75.7 and 71.5, respectively, in 2020 (Kementrian PPN/Bappenas et al. 2018b). This gender imbalance may bring further concerns as older women tend to be widowed (54.7 per cent), and older men tend to be married (82.7 per cent). Due to marriage and family responsibilities, many women do not participate in the labour market when they are in the working-age population, resulting in their old-age financial vulnerability. Regardless of gender, older persons were mainly married (60.9 per cent), followed by widowed (35.8 per cent), divorced (2.3 per cent), and single or never married (1.0 per cent).

Older persons can also be differentiated in their accessibility to infrastructure and public services. Here, the accessibility is indicated on whether they lived in urban or rural areas. There were more older persons residing in urban areas in 2018 than in 2020. This might reflect the rapid urbanization throughout the country. On the other hand, in 2018, rural population ageing was 9.9 per cent, higher than urban population ageing, 8.7 per cent. The higher rural than urban population ageing may indicate more challenges for rural older persons to get access to infrastructure and public services.

The older persons in 2018 were born before 1958. When they reached the schooling age, access to education was still limited, and hence the majority have low educational attainment. Our calculation shows that older persons in 2018 had a relatively low level of education. The older persons with at most primary education (including no education) accounted for more than 75 per cent of the total population of older persons. On the other hand, those with tertiary education comprised a very small percentage, only 3.8 per cent.

At the same time, the Indonesian economy is still dominated by informal sectors, hence most older persons in Indonesia cannot rely on pensions to finance their old ages. Furthermore, the government pension is only available to civil servants, military and police, and the amount of pension payout is meagre (Ananta, Arifin, and Moeis 2021). There is only a very limited pension system in the formal sectors. Therefore, combined with the disappearing filial piety and extended family system, most older persons need to continue working to support their own financial needs. Indeed, this chapter finds that 49.4 per cent of older persons were still working. Many worked in relatively more flexible sectors such as agriculture (28.6 per cent) and services (15.5 per cent). Only 5.3 per cent worked in manufacturing. Based on employment status, many worked in the informal sector, consisting of self-employed workers (17.7 per cent), employers assisted by temporary workers or unpaid workers (12.5 per cent), casual workers (5.1 per cent), and unpaid workers (5.2 per cent). Only 8.9 per cent were absorbed in the formal sector, which is defined as employees (6.4 per cent) or employers with paid workers (2.5 per cent). These statistics indicate a challenging time for many older persons who may still need to work for survival during the COVID-19 pandemic, especially in the informal sector or agriculture, when health protocols are relatively strict.

MAGNITUDE AND PREVALENCE OF OLDER PERSONS WITH HEARING DISABILITIES

Our findings show that nationally there were about 5.3 million Indonesian older persons experiencing some degree of hearing disability in 2018. This relatively large number of older persons with hearing disabilities may have resulted in greater employment and public health challenges during the COVID-19 pandemic. Relevant policies to minimize hearing capability deprivation among them not only will help improve their quality of life but will also empower them to remain contributing economically and socially to society.

In particular, among the 5.3 million, about 4 million experienced mild hearing disability and the rest experienced moderate or severe hearing disability. Many persons with mild hearing disabilities can still communicate without any hearing aid, especially in one-to-one communication in a quiet place. The overall prevalence rate among older persons was about 21.7 per cent, meaning that there were about 22 persons experiencing some degree of hearing disability per 100 older persons. This prevalence consists of 16.5 per cent of mild hearing disability and 5.2 per cent of moderate or severe hearing disability. Nevertheless, the overall prevalence is much higher than the calculated 12.7 per cent in 2010[6] based on the published data by Badan Pusat Statistik (2010). This rising prevalence, if not slowed down, may worsen the capability of the future older persons (current younger persons) to contribute to society.

Yet, the prevalence varies by demographic diversity such as age and sex. The prevalence significantly increased with age and accelerated after aged 65—regardless of the degree of hearing disability and sex (see Table 9.1). Older women had a higher prevalence of moderate or severe hearing disability than older men in all age groups (see Figure 9.1). In other words, older women have greater challenges in their daily communication than older men, partly because women live longer than men, indicating a sex paradox between higher life expectancy and worsening hearing disability among older women.

TABLE 9.1
Prevalence of Older Persons' Hearing Disability by Personal Characteristics: Indonesia, 2018

Variable	Moderate & Severe	Mild	No difficulty	X^2 test
Age				
60–64	1.67	8.61	89.72	$p < 0.001$
65–69	2.95	13.38	83.67	
70–74	5.85	22.12	72.03	
75–79	10.18	27.18	62.63	
80–84	16.93	34.18	48.89	
85–89	20.43	35.29	44.28	
90+	29.90	38.71	31.39	
Sex				
Male	4.53	15.10	80.36	$p < 0.001$
Female	5.83	17.69	76.48	
Marital status				
Married	3.43	13.24	83.32	$p < 0.001$
Single	7.24	15.32	77.44	
Divorced	5.70	15.45	78.85	
Widowed	8.14	22.02	69.83	
Educational attainment				
No education/less than primary	7.29	19.97	72.73	$p < 0.001$
Primary school	3.41	14.26	82.33	
Junior HS	3.16	11.83	85.01	
Senior HS	1.90	10.04	88.06	
Tertiary education	1.17	7.35	91.48	
Place of residence				
Urban	4.57	15.33	80.11	$p < 0.001$
Rural	5.90	17.67	76.43	

Note: HS = High school
Source: Authors' calculation based on the 2018 SUSENAS raw data.

The prevalence of hearing disability also varies by marital status. Married older persons are found to have better hearing than other marital statuses (see Table 9.1). Widows have the highest prevalence of hearing disability. Stress from the death of a spouse and the resulting change in ways of life may be associated with hearing disability.

The earlier discussion shows an increasing trend of overall hearing disabilities among older persons. In addition, Table 9.1 indicates a significant positive association between education and hearing disability—the higher the education, the lower is the prevalence of hearing disability. However, this trend may be slowed down because the education of currently younger persons (future older persons) is rising.

FIGURE 9.1
Prevalence of Hearing Disability by Age and Sex: Indonesia, 2018

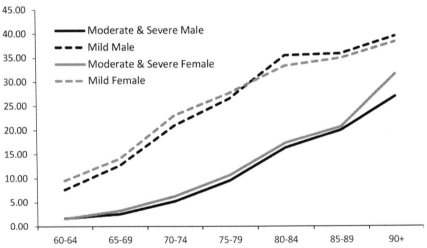

Source: Authors' calculation.

Environmental condition is also important in affecting older persons' hearing capability deprivation. Two environmental variables are considered here: urban-rural residence and province. Older persons living in urban areas were more likely to have better hearing than those living in rural areas for whatever the degree of hearing disability (see Table 9.1). The prevalence of moderate or severe hearing disability in rural areas was higher than that in urban areas, giving more challenges to empower rural older persons with hearing disability. The high cost and limited availability of hearing aids in rural areas may further worsen the hearing capability deprivation of rural older persons.

Moreover, the prevalence also varies among provinces. High prevalence of hearing disability is not necessarily found in provinces with old population structure (population with older persons accounting for more than 12 per cent); it is also seen in provinces with young population structure (population with older persons accounting for less than 7 per cent). For example, the province of Gorontalo has young population structure, but it has the highest prevalence of hearing disability among older persons in Indonesia (28.7 per cent) (see Table 9.2). Yet, the lowest prevalence, 16.6 per cent, is also found in a province with young population structure—Riau Province. It is therefore important to pay attention to the regional diversity on hearing disabilities, regardless the population age structure.

TABLE 9.2
Provincial Prevalence of Older Persons with Hearing Disability: Indonesia, 2018

No.	Province	Degree Moderate & Severe	Mild	No difficulty
1	Aceh	6.17	19.07	74.75
2	North Sumatra	4.57	19.32	76.11
3	West Sumatra	4.95	15.26	79.79
4	Riau	5.53	18.24	76.23
5	Jambi	5.72	16.04	78.24
6	South Sumatra	6.39	18.68	74.93
7	Bengkulu	5.82	21.14	73.04
8	Lampung	5.64	15.61	78.75
9	Bangka Belitung	4.54	14.65	80.82
10	Riau Archipelago	4.06	12.56	83.38
11	Jakarta	3.36	13.90	82.74
12	West Java	5.07	15.90	79.04
13	Central Java	5.50	16.10	78.40

TABLE 9.2 (continued)

14	Yogyakarta	6.04	13.25	80.71
15	East Java	4.68	15.50	79.82
16	Banten	6.62	17.83	75.55
17	Bali	3.64	16.05	80.30
18	West Nusa Tenggara	6.10	16.88	77.02
19	East Nusa Tenggara	6.79	19.17	74.04
20	West Kalimantan	6.11	21.87	72.02
21	Central Kalimantan	4.75	18.03	77.22
22	South Kalimantan	4.36	16.72	78.92
23	East Kalimantan	4.73	17.54	77.74
24	North Kalimantan	7.28	18.11	74.60
25	North Sulawesi	4.67	12.60	82.74
26	Central Sulawesi	7.19	18.61	74.19
27	South Sulawesi	6.31	20.78	72.90
28	Southeast Sulawesi	4.75	15.95	79.30
29	Gorontalo	7.04	21.61	71.35
30	West Sulawesi	6.25	17.50	76.25
31	Maluku	3.83	13.36	82.81
32	North Maluku	5.69	14.07	80.23
33	West Papua	3.94	15.42	80.64
34	Papua	2.32	15.87	81.81
	Indonesia	5.21	16.46	78.33

Notes: We use the weighted sample to provide national and provincial estimates. The weighted sample covers 24,494,103 older persons.

Source: Authors' calculation based on the 2018 SUSENAS raw data.

HEARING DISABILITIES AND QUALITY OF LIFE

Quality of life is a multidimensional concept. It is defined by World Health Organization as "individuals' perceptions of their position in life in the context of the culture and value systems in which they live and in relation to their goals, expectations, standards and concerns" (WHO 1998, p. 2). It encompasses six domains: physical, psychological, social, level of independence, environment, and spirituality/religion/personal beliefs. In this section, the quality of life of older persons with hearing disabilities is indicated by variables belonging to several dimensions such as employment, health status, the quality of communication and emotion, as well as access to digital technology.

Employment

Employment is categorized under the domain of level of independence of WHO Quality of Life (WHO 1998). Our findings show that about one in two older persons in Indonesia were still working in their old age. As often found, they were employed in the informal sector, and were mainly engaged in the primary sector or agriculture (see Table 9.3). Flexibility and openness in these sectors might help them to economically participate in the labour market.

Their participation in the labour market is associated with the degree of hearing disability. The higher the degree of hearing disability, the smaller was the percentage of working older persons in the informal sector, unpaid work and formal sector (see Table 9.3). Older persons with a moderate or severe hearing disability had the highest percentage

TABLE 9.3
Older Persons' Hearing Disability and Employment: Indonesia, 2018

Hearing Disability	Informal	Formal	Unpaid	Not working	Total
Moderate & Severe	16.79	3.05	1.86	78.29	100.00
Mild	25.51	4.47	4.05	65.96	100.00
No difficulty	38.65	10.14	5.70	45.50	100.00
Total	35.35	8.84	5.23	50.58	100.00
Hearing Disability	Agriculture	Manufacturing	Services	Not working	
Moderate & Severe	13.76	2.36	5.59	78.29	100.00
Mild	22.71	2.69	8.65	65.96	100.00
No difficulty	30.89	5.99	17.62	45.50	100.00
Total	28.65	5.26	15.51	50.58	100.00

Source: Authors' calculation based on the 2018 SUSENAS raw data.

of not working among other groups (mild disability or no disability). Almost eight in ten older persons with a moderate or severe hearing disability were not working, compared to seven and five non-working older persons with mild and no difficulty at all in hearing disability, respectively. Therefore, there were older persons with hearing disability who were still able to work.

In each degree of hearing difficulty, working older persons were mainly involved in the informal sector as compared to the formal sector or unpaid work. In addition, based on the industry, older persons mainly work in agriculture, followed by service sectors and manufacturing industries regardless of the degree of hearing disability. This finding corroborates with earlier studies (Arifin and Ananta 2009; Ananta 2014) that older persons are more likely to work in the informal sectors and agriculture.

The national minimum wage in 2018 was 2.29 million rupiahs per month.[7] Older persons working in the informal sector or agricultural industry receive wages, on average, lower than the minimum wage. Badan Pusat Statistik (2018) reported that older persons received 1.19 million rupiahs per month in 2018, or 52.0 per cent of the minimum wage. Therefore, the older persons with hearing disabilities may have also suffered more in financing themselves through employment relative to those without any disabilities.

The health protocols during a pandemic such as the COVID-19 may even worsen their hearing capability deprivation, resulting in less likelihood to work and support their own life. They possibly depend on others to support them financially and are unable to contribute economically and socially to society. Therefore, older persons with moderate to severe hearing disabilities may have been mostly deprived of participation in the labour market during this pandemic.

Health Status

Health status belongs to the physical domain of WHO Quality of Life. Older persons, in general, may not be in good health. In 2018, more than half (51.3 per cent) were not in their primary health as they experienced certain health complaints. Furthermore, 26.3 per cent were sick and their daily activities were disrupted, while 25.3 per cent were in good health.

Hearing disability may also be associated with health status. The likelihood of being healthy among those with moderate or severe hearing disabilities was much lower (36.0 per cent) than those without hearing disability (51.64 per cent). Those with a mild hearing disability had only a slightly higher percentage of being healthy (38.6 per cent).

Moreover, the degree of hearing disability is also associated with a disruption in daily activities. Older persons with a higher degree of hearing disability were more likely to experience disrupted daily activities when they were not in good health. About 42.6 per cent of older persons with moderate or severe hearing disability experience disrupted daily activities when they were not in good health, compared to 34.9 per cent of older persons with mild hearing disability. However, among those without hearing disability, only 23.0 per cent experienced a disruption in their daily activities when they reported not being in good health.

These findings imply that those with hearing disability may have worsening health and more disrupted daily activities during the COVID-19 pandemic. Indeed, the health status of older persons may have deteriorated during the COVID-19 pandemic. The health deterioration is also associated with their economic condition in which older persons who experience a decline in income are more likely to experience health deterioration than others who have the same income or increased income (Study Team 2021).

Communication and Emotion

Persons with hearing disabilities face some other challenging capability deprivations, including communication and emotion. These deprivations can be worsened by health protocols operating during the COVID-19 pandemic. Older persons with hearing disability face even more significant challenges in communication. Even before the pandemic, in 2018, almost 10 out of 100 older persons experienced communication difficulties. Among older persons with moderate or severe hearing disability, 30.3 per cent experienced moderate or severe disability in communication, and 27.1 per cent experienced mild disability in communication. This is in contrast to older persons without hearing disability (see Table 9.4). Older persons with mild hearing disability were in between these two groups. In other words, older persons with a higher degree of hearing disability is more likely to be accompanied with higher difficulty in communication.

Communication for persons with hearing disability may have also been more challenging during the COVID-19 pandemic when they access public services. An illustration is a case of a bank customer with hearing disability in Indonesia in the early months of the COVID-19 pandemic in 2020. This customer is a lady asking for a special request. She requested the bank staff, who wore a facial mask, to conduct written communication through a piece of paper as she experienced difficulty reading the staff's lips.[8] Therefore, written communication helps minimize capability deprivation in communication. Another alternative to minimize the capability deprivation is a clear, transparent facial mask to reduce hearing capability deprivation.

Barriers to communication may lead to poor psychological well-being, such as the ability to control emotion. Naylor, Burke and Holman (2020) found that greater anxiety was observed among people with hearing disability when they spoke with people wearing facial masks in public spaces such as malls, markets, or parks. Our data shows that most older persons in Indonesia did not have any problem controlling

TABLE 9.4
Older Persons Hearing Disability with Difficulty in Communication and Difficulty in Controlling Emotion: Indonesia, 2018

Hearing Disability	Difficulty in Communication			
	Moderate or Severe	Mild	Normal	Total
Moderate or Severe	30.30	27.06	42.64	100.00
Mild	3.63	21.95	74.42	100.00
No hearing disability	0.74	1.99	97.27	100.00
Total	2.76	6.59	90.66	100.00

	Difficulty in Emotion			
Hearing Disability	Moderate or Severe	Mild	Normal	Total
Moderate or Severe	15.81	19.42	64.77	100.00
Mild	3.09	16.60	80.31	100.00
No hearing disability	0.87	2.78	96.35	100.00
Total	2.01	5.92	92.06	100.00

Source: Authors' calculation based on the 2018 SUSENAS raw data.

their emotions. Only 2 per cent of older persons experienced moderate or severe difficulty in controlling emotion (see Table 9.4). This table shows that hearing disability has a better association with emotion than with communication. Only 15.8 per cent of those having moderate or severe hearing disability experienced moderate or severe difficulty in controlling emotion.

Table 9.4 also implies that some older persons may suffer from triple capability deprivations: hearing capability deprivation, communication capability deprivation, and emotion control capability deprivation. Indeed, further calculation (not shown in the table) reveals that 3.4 per cent of older persons experienced these triple disabilities. They are the ones who suffer from low quality of life and they deserve serious attention and decent life, especially during the COVID-19 pandemic.

Access to Digital Technology

Digital technology has rapidly advanced, with a rising concern on the digital gap between the young and old population. New communication technologies such as smartphones, computers or tablets, and the internet have penetrated everybody's life. Unfortunately, the use of these technologies among older persons is still limited. Yet, the accessibility and affordability of these technologies can minimize the capability deprivation in communication and emotion faced by people with hearing disability.

Our data provide empirical evidence on the extent of the access to digital technology such as handphones or smartphones, computers and the internet among older persons in Indonesia. Only 2.6 per cent of older persons in 2018 used computers. Badan Pusat Statistik (2020) indicated declining percentage of computer users among older persons to 1.5 per cent in 2020. On the other hand, the use of handphones among older persons has increased from 41.8 per cent in 2018, before the COVID-19 pandemic, to 46.7 per cent in 2020 during the pandemic. At the same time, internet users among older persons have also risen from 5.7 per cent in 2018 to 11.4 per cent in 2020. Therefore, the use of handphones or smartphones may have replaced the use of computers among older persons during the current pandemic.

Nevertheless, taking into account the degree of hearing disability, there were only very few older persons with a moderate or severe hearing disability who used computers or the internet (0.25 per cent and 0.73 per cent, respectively). Among older persons with mild hearing disability, only almost one in 100 used a computer and 1.8 per cent used the internet. Meanwhile, even among those without any difficulty at all in hearing, only three in 100 older persons used computers and 6.9 per cent used the internet. This may indicate that older persons with hearing disability are deprived from the accessibility and affordability of such technologies. In other words, technology may not have covered their needs in minimizing their hearing capability deprivation.

Although only about half of older persons used mobile phones, these devices might have helped them to communicate, especially those with hearing disabilities. Not only they minimize the risk of virus transmission, but as argued in Banskota et al. (2020), the use of the mobile phone can reduce feelings of loneliness and isolation. During the COVID-19 pandemic, when physical meetings and communication are limited, the use of the mobile phone has enabled virtual meetings between persons having hearing disabilities and their family members. Nevertheless, the data show a paradox: only 30.4 per cent of the older persons owned a mobile phone, even though the gadget may help them in communication, especially for those with hearing disabilities. Technology gaps and financial limitations may have prevented them from owning, learning and using the new gadget.

Furthermore, 47.0 per cent of older persons without hearing disability used a mobile phone, which is higher than among those with hearing disability. Persons with mild hearing disability were more likely to own and use the gadget. On average, among 100 older persons experiencing moderate or severe disability, only 13 persons used mobile phones, much smaller than 27 per 100 people with mild hearing disability. Similarly, the ownership of mobile phone was less among older persons with moderate and severe hearing disability (7.7 per cent) compared to those with mild hearing disability (16.7 per cent). The result may imply the need to introduce older persons to digital technology and to create older-persons friendly digital technology, including communication tools such as mobile phones.

CONCLUSION

This chapter shows that older persons with hearing disabilities in Indonesia are significant in number and prevalence. At the same time, the absolute number and prevalence have been rising and may continue to rise as Indonesia is undergoing a deepening population ageing, indicated by a rising number and percentage of older persons. The percentage of the oldest old (aged 80 years old and over) will also rise. The COVID-19 pandemic came unprecedentedly and has worsened the hearing capability deprivation of this vulnerable group. During the pandemic, persons with hearing disability may experience triple difficulties—in hearing, communicating, and controlling emotion.

Hearing capability deprivation among older persons in Indonesia may not only result in their lower quality of life but also disempowers them economically and socially. The hearing capability deprivation and vulnerability of persons with hearing disability also vary by demographic characteristics.

Therefore, recommendations can be made in three areas, which should be implemented simultaneously. As hearing disability may happen progressively to anybody, the first recommendation is to delay the onset of the hearing disability. Once the hearing disability has started, the second recommendation is to slow down the progression of hearing disability. Given the irreversibility of the disability, the third recommendation is to minimize the existing hearing capability deprivation.

NOTES

1. Many studies have then applied the capability approach to various topics. Following are just a few examples. Mitra et al. (2011) examined the relationship between disability and poverty; Lavie-Ajayi et al. (2018) applied the capabilities approach to understanding public services for people with mental disabilities. Trani et al. (2018) estimated disability using the capability deprivation approach. Bonaccio et al. (2020) studied how people with disabilities participated in workplaces.
2. See Tahden et al. (2018) for more discussion on using hearing aids.
3. "See Through Solution: Deaf Indonesians Turn to Clear Coronavirus Masks to Help Lip Reading". *Straits Times*, 28 April 2020. https://www.straitstimes.com/asia/se-asia/see-through-solution-deaf-indonesians-turn-to-clear-coronavirus-masks (accessed 30 April 2021).
4. "Masker Transparan Buatan Wonogiri bagi Tunarungu". *Media Indonesia*, 1 May 2020. https://mediaindonesia.com/nusantara/309365/masker-transparan-buatan-wonogiri-bagi-tunar ungu. In this report, Sutantini is a tailor and deaf. "Masker Transparan Karya Penyandang Tuli dari

Wonogiri". *Kompas*, 5 May 2020. https://www.kompas.com/tren/read/2020/05/05/081700565/masker-transparan-karya-penyandang-tuli-dari-wonogiri?page=all#page2 (accessed 30 April 2021).
5. Transparent mask was produced locally driven by the difficulties in daily communication faced by people with hearing disabilities. It is produced to be shared with others who have the same difficulty in hearing. "Difabel Bertahan di Tengah Pandemic Covid-19, Sulit Jaga Jarak Sosial hingga Penghasilan Berkurang". *Kompas*, 24 April 2020. https://regional.kompas.com/read/2020/04/24/17180081/difabel-bertahan-di-tengah-pandemi-covid-19-sulit-jaga-jarak-sosial-hingga (accessed 30 April 2021).
6. The prevalence was calculated based on the official information provided by the 2010 population census in this site. "Penduduk Menurut Kelompok Umur dan Tingkat Kesulitan Mendengar Indonesia". Badan Pusat Statistik, undated. https://sp2010.bps.go.id/index.php/site/tabel?tid=275&wid=0. About 2.3 million older people experienced some degree of hearing loss. The total population aged 60 years and above numbered 18.0 million.
7. "Upah Minimum Regional/Propinsi (Rupiah), 2018-2020". Badan Pusat Statistik, undated. https://www.bps.go.id/indicator/19/220/1/upah-minimum-regional-propinsi.html (accessed 29 April 2022).
8. "People with Disabilities Demand Access to Information Basic Rights during Pandemic". *Jakarta Post*, 12 June 2020. https://www.thejakartapost.com/news/2020/06/12/people-with-disabilities-demand-access-to-information-basic-rights-during-pandemic.html (accessed 30 April 2021).

REFERENCES

Alqudah, Safa, Maha Zaitoun, Ola Alqudah, Sara Alqudah and Zainab Alqudah. 2021. "Challenges Facing Users of Hearing Aids during the COVID-19 Pandemic". *International Journal of Audiology* 60, no. 10: 747–53. https://doi.org/10.1080/14992027.2021.1872806.

Ananta, Aris. 2014. "Employment Patterns of Older Women in Indonesia 2007". In *Gender and Ageing in Southeast Asia*, edited by Theresa Devasahayam. Singapore: Institute of Southeast Asian Studies.

Arifin, Evi Nurvidya and Aris Ananta. 2009. "Employment of Older Persons: Diversity across Nations and Sub-Nations in Southeast Asia". In *Older Persons in Southeast Asia: an Emerging Asset*, edited by Evi Nurvidya Arifin and Aris Ananta. Singapore: Institute of Southeast Asian Studies.

Badan Penelitian dan Pengembangan Kesehatan. 2019. *Laporan Nasional Riskesdas 2018*. Jakarta: Lembaga Penerbit, Badan Penelitian dan Pengembangan Kesehatan.

Badan Pusat Statistik. 2018. *Keadaan Pekerja di Indonesia Agustus 2018*. Jakarta: Badan Pusat Statistik.

———. 2020. *Statistik Penduduk Lanjut Usia 2020*. Jakarta: Badan Pusat Statistik.

Banskota, Swechya, Margaret Healy and Elizabeth M. Goldberg. 2020. "15 Smartphone Apps for Older Adults to Use While in Isolation during the COVID-19 Pandemic". *Western Journal of Emergency Medicine* 21, no. 3: 514–25.

Bonaccio, Silvia, Catherine E. Connelly, Ian R. Gellatly, Arif Jetha, and Kathleen A. Martin Ginis. 2020. "The Participation of People with Disabilities in the Workplace across the Employment Cycle: Employer Concerns and Research Evidence". *Journal of Business and Psychology* 35: 135–58.

Groce, Nora E. and Daniel Mont. 2017. "Counting Disability: Emerging Consensus on the Washington Group Questionnaire". *Lancet* 5: e649–e650.

Hulzen, Richard D. Ten and David A. Fabry. 2020. "Impact of Hearing Loss and Universal Face Masking in the COVID-19 Era". *Mayo Clin Proc* 95, no. 10: 2069–72. https://doi.org/10.1016/j.mayocp.2020.07.027.

Kementrian PPN/Bappenas, BPS-Statistics Indonesia and UNFPA. 2018a. *Indonesia Population Projection: Results of SUPAS 2015*. Jakarta: Badan Pusat Statistik.

———. 2018b. *Indonesian Population Projection 2015-2045*. Jakarta: Kementrian PPN/Bappenas, BPS-Statistics Indonesia and UNFPA.

Lavie-Ajayi, Maya, Gallia S. Moran, Itzhak Levav, Rotem Porat, Tal Reches, Margalit Goldfracht, and Gilad Gal. 2018. "Using the *Capabilities Approach* to Understand Inequality in Primary Health-care Services for People with Severe Mental Illness". *Israel Journal of Health Policy Research* 7, no. 49.

McDaid, David, A-La Park and Shelly Chadha. 2021. "Estimating the Global Costs of Hearing Loss". *International Journal of Audiology* 60, no. 3: 162–70. https://doi.org/10.1080/14992027.2021.1883197.

Mitra, Sophie, Aleksandra Posarac and Brandon Vick. 2011. "Disability and Poverty in Developing Countries: A Snapshot from the World Health Survey". *SP DISCUSSION PAPER* 1109. Washington, D.C.: The World Bank Social Protection and Labor.

Nuesse, Theresa, Anne Schlueter, Ulrike Lemke and Inga Holube. 2021. "Self-reported Hearing Handicap in Adults Aged 55 to 81 Years is Modulated by Hearing Abilities, Frailty, Mental Health, and Willingness to Use Hearing Aids". *International Journal of Audiology* 60: 71–79. https://doi.org/10.1080/14992027.2020.1858237.

Sen, Amartya. 2000. *Development as Freedom*. New York: Afred A. Knopf.

———. 2009. *The Idea of Justice*. London: Allen Lane.

Sher, Taimur, Greta C. Stamper, and Larry B. Lundy. 2020. "COVID-19 and Vulnerable Population with Communication Disorders". *Mayo Clin Proc.* 95, no. 9: 1845–47.

Study Team. 2021. "Health". In *Older People and COVID-19 in Indonesia*, edited by Komazawa, O., N.W. Suriastini, I.Y. Wijayanti, Maliki and D.D. Kharisma, pp. 40–63. Jakarta: ERIA and Bappenas; Yogyakarta: SurveyMETER.

Tahden, Maike A.S., Anja Gieseler, Markus Meis, Kirsten C. Wagener, and Hans Colonius. 2018. "What Keeps Older Adults with Hearing Impairment from Adopting Hearing Aids?" *Trends in Hearing* 22: 1–17.

Trani, Jean-Francois, Parul Bakhshi, Derek Brown, Dominique Lopez, and Fional Gall. 2018. "Disability as Deprivation of Capabilities: Estimation using a Large-scale Survey in Morocco and Tunisia and an Instrumental Variable Approach". *Social Science & Medicine* 211: 48–60.

Trecca, Eleonora M.C., Matteo Gelardi, and Michele Cassano. 2020. "COVID-19 and Hearing Difficulties". *Am J Otolaryngol* 41: 102496.

World Health Organisation (WHO). 1998. *WHOQOL User Manual*. Geneva: WHO.

───── . 2021. *World Report on Hearing*. Geneva: WHO.

INDEX

A
abuse, 41, 57, 62, 75
access to credit, 110
accommodation, 32–33, 122, 129. See also shelters
acculturation, 68–70, 72–81, 86–89, 93–96
adaptive capacities, 102–5, 107, 109–17
admission into local schools, 88–92
ageing. See older persons
Anderson, Benedict, 78
anti-foreigner sentiments, 86–87, 93–96
anxiety, 160
antigen rapid testing (ART), 40
ASEAN markets, 71–72
Asian financial crisis, 107
asset-building, 134. See also property ownership
assistance, disbursement of, 102–7, 109–16, 130

B
Badan Pusat Statistik, 145, 150
Batam, 123

births, 13, 16–17, 86. See also deaths; fertility
borders
  closure of, 30–34, 121–22, 124, 132–33, 136
  crossings of (see cross-border commuting)
  relationships across, 31–38
  reopening of, 38–40, 65n3
brokers, 53, 59–60, 64, 95–96
Buddhist organizations, 74

C
capability deprivation
  demographic diversity, 147, 150–56
  physical environment, 147, 149, 154–56
  social infrastructure, 147, 151
  social norms, 147–48
  See also hearing disabilities; older persons
capital, lack of access to, 110
care work, 24, 34, 69
cash transfers, 103, 112–15, 117
Causeway, 29
Central Provident Fund (CPF), 130, 137n1

Child Support Grant (CSG), 113, 116
children
  number of, 13, 16–17
  protection of, 107, 109–17
Chinese immigrants, 93–94
Christian churches, 74
"Circuit Breaker", 31, 122, 124
citizenship, 38, 52. *See also* naturalization
City Square Mall (Johor Bahru), 36
civil society support services, 74–75
climate change, 104, 106, 110. *See also* disaster impacts; floods
cohabitation, 14–15
Committee for Overseas Vietnamese Affairs, 74
communication difficulties, 148–49, 159–61. *See also* hearing disabilities
community building, 77–79, 81. *See also* "enclave societies"
Compassionate Travel Scheme, 39
competition
  in common spaces, 86–96
  displaced by, 127–35
computers, 161–62
contributory benefits, 103–4, 109, 112–17
coping mechanisms. *See* social protection
co-residence, 17. *See also* migration
cosmopolitanism, 73, 122
cost of living, 36–37, 123, 129–32
COVID-19 pandemic
  challenges faced during, 157–62
  effects of, 92, 144–45
  health protocols (*see* health protocols)
  hearing disability during, 148–49
  homelessness during (*see* homelessness)
  immigration policy impacted by, 85
  livelihoods affected during, 31–34, 37–38, 43
  lockdowns, 30–34, 121–22, 124, 132–33, 136
  "new normal", 41–44
  Singapore's/Malaysia's situation of, 31–34, 38–40, 121, 122, 124
  social protection programmes during, 112–17
  testing for, 40, 65n3, 121, 133
  vaccinations, 39–40, 65n3
  See also economic precarity
COVID-19 variants, 31, 39–40, 44n7
CPF (Central Provident Fund), 130, 137n1
credit access, 110
crop insurance, 104, 110
cross-border commuting
  housing insecurity and, 127–35
  prohibition of, 30–34, 121–22, 124, 132, 136
  reallowing of, 38–40, 65n3
  relationships in, 31–38, 42–43
  See also borders; mobility; Singapore-Malaysia connection
cross-national marriages. *See* foreign marriages
CSG (Child Support Grant), 113, 116
cultural adaptation, 68–70, 72–81, 86–89, 93–96

D

daily activities, disruption in, 159
day trips, 36–37. *See also* cross-border commuting
deaths, 14, 17, 24, 33, 41, 111–12. *See also* births
Delta variant, 31, 39–40
demographic changes
  births, 13, 16–17, 86

Index

deaths, 14, 17, 24, 33, 41, 111–12
differences between countries, 54–55
divorces, 15–16, 20, 62, 74, 134
employment (*see* employment)
family structure impacted by, 16–20
fertility, 13, 16–17, 41, 54, 61, 86
gender imbalance, 24, 150, 152
marriages (*see* marriages)
migration (*see* migration)
demographic diversity, 147, 150–56
demographic transition theory, 54, 64n1
deprivation
  during COVID-19 pandemic, 112–17
  hearing disabilities as (*see* capability deprivation)
  and social protection, 102–5, 107, 109–12
  See also economic precarity; poverty
diasporic populations, 73, 122
digital technology, 161–62
disabilities. *See* hearing disabilities
discrimination, 148. *See also* hearing aids
disaster impacts, 106–7. *See also* climate change
disaster risk management (DRM). *See* social protection
distancing from family, 127–29, 136. *See also* family relationships
diversity in society, 86–91, 95. *See also* inequalities; integration into society
divorces, 15–16, 20, 62, 74, 134. *See also* marriages
documented workers, 58–63
domestic violence, 41, 57, 62, 75
DRM (disaster risk management). *See* social protection

E

economic inequalities, 52, 57–58, 64, 103–4, 115. *See also* diversity in society
economic precarity, 32–33, 85, 95, 112–13, 127–33, 158. *See also* COVID-19 pandemic; financial vulnerability; job insecurity; livelihoods; poverty
education
  hearing disabilities and, 154
  school systems (*see* school systems)
EduCity (Johor Bahru), 36
emergency assistance, 102–7, 109–15
emotion, controlling of, 159–61
employment
  hiring practices, 85–86
  interventions in, 102–5, 107, 109–11, 115–17
  of Malaysian workers in Singapore, 31–34, 37–38, 43
  older persons in, 151–52, 157–58
  opportunities in, 147–48
  See also unemployment
Employment Pass (EP), 85
Employment Permit System (EPS), 56–57, 59–62, 68–69
"enclave societies", 52, 72, 75, 95. *See also* community building
endemics, 38–40, 65n3
entertainment industry, 32
entrepreneurship, 110–11
EP (Employment Pass), 85
EPS (Employment Permit System), 56–57, 59–62, 68–69
estrangement, 127–29, 136. *See also* family relationships
expatriate families, 89, 91
expectation asymmetries, 69. *See also* foreign marriages
extracurricular activities, 76–77, 87

F

face masking, 148–49, 160
family relationships, 31–34, 42, 127–29, 136
family structure, 13, 16–23, 62
family suffering, 31–34, 42, 74, 122, 130–35, 144
family support, 17, 24
feminization of ageing, 24, 150, 152
fertility, 13, 16–17, 41, 54, 61, 86. *See also* older persons
financial assistance, 103–4, 109, 112, 116, 130
financial sectors, 85, 122
financial vulnerability, 129–33, 150, 158. *See also* economic precarity; poverty
floods, 106–7, 110, 112. *See also* climate change
foreign investments, 35, 37, 42–43, 44n4, 71–72
foreign labour
    demand for, 37–38, 51–54, 56–64, 68–69, 71
    difficulties encountered by, 31–34, 74–75, 120–22, 127–35
    teachers, foreign-born, 92–93
    support for families of, 69–70, 71, 74–81
    talents among, 85–87, 122
    types of, 44n3
foreign languages, 59, 64, 70, 73, 75–81. *See also* language barrier
foreign marriages
    demographic changes due to, 13–17
    difficulties encountered in, 57, 61–62, 74–75, 87, 123, 129–35
    preparation for, 69, 73, 75–81
    support for migrants of, 69, 74–79
foreign students, 68–69, 72, 80–81, 88–94
foreign talents, 85–87, 122

G

gender imbalance, 24, 150, 152. *See also* demographic changes
generational support, 17
getaways, 36–37. *See also* cross-border commuting
global householding, 13, 14–15, 17. *See also* households
global network, 91–92
global talents, 85–87, 122
globalization, 73
government support, 75–77, 91–92, 112–17, 121
grandparenthood, 17, 19. *See also* older persons

H

handphones, 161–62
hangul, 70, 76, 79. *See also* Korean language
HDB (Housing Development Board), 134, 138n2
health protocols
    face masking, 148–49, 160
    physical distancing, 148–49
    quarantine, 38–40, 65n3, 121, 133
    travel restrictions, 31, 32, 38–39, 121, 133
health status, 158–59. *See also* older persons
healthcare, 104, 111–12. *See also* social protection
hearing aids, 146–49
hearing disabilities
    as capability deprivation (*see* capability deprivation)
    communication difficulties and, 148–49, 159–61
    during COVID-19 pandemic, 148–49
    older persons with, 152–56

and quality of life, 156–62
  See also poverty
Hello Kitty Town (Johor Bahru), 36, 44n5
hiring practices, 85–86. *See also* employment
holidays, 36–37. *See also* cross-border commuting
homelessness
  defining, 124
  insecurity due to, 120–22, 127–35
  types of, 125, 136
hospitals, 149. *See also* physical environment
households
  demographic effects on, 13–16
  resilience of, 102–5, 107, 109–12, 115–17
  structure of, 16–23, 62
  See also demographic changes
housing
  arrangements for, 14–15, 17, 19, 20–23, 120–25
  insecurity due to, 32–33, 123, 127–35
  ownership of, 35, 37, 42–43, 44n4, 123, 133–35
Housing Development Board (HDB), 134, 138n2
Human Development Report, 104
humanitarian support, 102–5, 107, 109–17
Hyundai, 72

I

"imagined communities", 77–79, 81. *See also* "enclave societies"
immigration
  effects on education policy, 88–94
  enclaves due to, 52, 72, 75, 95
  policy of, 85–86
  rules of, 133–34
  See also migration; My Malaysia Second Home (MMSH) programme; translocality
income disparity, 52, 57–58, 64. *See also* economic inequalities
income losses, 129–33. *See also* economic precarity
income risks, 110–13, 115. *See also* livelihoods
Indian immigrants, 93–94
individual freedom, 146–48. *See also* capability deprivation
Indonesia
  Batam, 123
  face masking in, 149
  living in, 129–35
  older persons in, 150–56
inequalities, 35, 38, 52, 57–58, 64, 103–4, 115. *See also* diversity in society
infant mortality rates, 111–12. *See also* healthcare
infections, 31, 39–40, 121, 144. *See also* COVID-19 pandemic
informal debts, 110
informal sector
  employment in, 151–52, 157–58
  insecurity of working in, 107, 112–13, 115–16, 130–33
information asymmetries, 69. *See also* foreign marriages
in-kind transfers, 103, 112–15, 117
insurance schemes, 104, 110
integration into society, 68–70, 72–81, 86–96, 134. *See also* diversity in society; social cohesion
inter-cultural awareness, 91–93. *See also* diversity in society
intermediaries, 53, 59–60, 64, 95–96
international marriages. *See* foreign marriages

International Organization for Migration, 69
international students, 68–69, 72, 80–81, 88–94
internet users, 161–62
isolation, 127–29, 136. See also family relationships

J
job insecurity, 85, 95, 124, 130–33. See also economic precarity
Johor Bahru-Singapore connection. See Singapore-Malaysia connection
Joint Singles Scheme, 134. See also housing

K
Kakao app, 77, 81n2. See also community building
khon phi (ghost people), 59. See also foreign labour
Korean culture, 58, 70
Korean language, 59, 64, 70, 73, 75–81
Korean universities, 72

L
labour contracts, 74–75
labour market, 103–4, 115, 157–58
labourers. See foreign labour
language barrier, 73, 75–81, 92–93. See also foreign languages
less fortunate, 102–5, 107, 109–17
life expectancy, 14, 17, 24, 150. See also demographic changes
life trajectories
 barriers to housing, 134–35
 insecure work, 85, 95, 124, 130–33
 poverty, 33, 127–32
 relationships breakdown, 127–29, 136

unemployment, 115, 124, 130, 131, 133
violence, 41, 57, 62, 75
lifestyle choices, 122–23
linguistic training, 73, 75–81. See also language barrier
lip reading, 148–49, 160. See also hearing disabilities
livelihoods
 COVID-19's effects on, 31–34, 37–38, 43
 diversification of, 102–5, 107, 109–11, 115–17
 housing arrangements affected by, 129–32
 See also economic precarity; income risks
living arrangements, 14–15, 17, 19, 20–23, 120–25. See also housing
living expenses, 36–37, 123, 129–32
local-foreigner divide, 86–87, 93–96. See also integration into society
local students, 93–94
local teachers, 92–93
local workforce, 85–87
lockdowns, 30–34, 121–22, 124, 132–33, 136
long-term residence, 125, 133. See also shelters
losing touch, 127–28, 136. See also family relationships
lower-income persons, 33, 127–32. See also poor people

M
mainstream schooling. See school systems
Makassar (Indonesia), 149
makeshift housing arrangements. See homelessness
Malaysia
 Johor Bahru, 36

Index

living in, 129–35
Movement Control Order (MCO), 31, 32, 121
and Singapore connection (*see* Singapore-Malaysia connection)
manpower policy (Singapore), 33, 85–86
marital status, 134, 154
marriages
  demographic changes due to, 13–17
  difficulties encountered in, 57, 61–62, 74–75, 87, 123, 129–35
  dissolution of, 15–16, 20, 62, 74, 134
  preparation for, 69, 73, 75–81
  support for migrants of foreign, 69, 74–79
Mass Rapid Transit (MRT), 33, 44n2
matrimonial flats, 134. *See also* housing
MCO (Movement Control Order), 31, 32, 121
medical schemes, 104, 111–12. *See also* social protection
mental health, 121, 159–61
migrant families, 69–70, 71, 74–81
migrant labour. *See* foreign labour
migration
  across countries, 13, 17, 19, 20, 78, 121–22, 127–35
  histories of, 70–71
  reasons for, 51–54, 57–64, 68–70
  replacement, 88, 93–94
  See also immigration; My Malaysia Second Home (MMSH) programme; translocality
minimum wages, 158. *See also* employment
Ministry of Education, Singapore, 87–89, 91–93
Ministry of Foreign Affairs, Vietnam, 74

MMSH (My Malaysia Second Home) programme, 35, 37, 42–43, 44n4
mobile phones, 161–62
mobility, 34–38, 41–42, 121–24, 127–35. *See also* cross-border commuting
Monetary Authority of Singapore, 86
monkeypox virus, 44n7
Moon Jae-in, 71–72
mortality, 14, 17, 24, 33, 41, 111–12. *See also* births
Movement Control Order (MCO), 31, 32, 121
MRT (Mass Rapid Transit), 33, 44n2
multiculturalism
  families of, 69–70, 71, 74–81
  marriages of (*see* foreign marriages)
  in schools, 86–89, 93–96
My Malaysia Second Home (MMSH) programme, 35, 37, 42–43, 44n4

N

national identity, 87, 122
National Integration Council (NIC), 88
National Social and Economic Survey (SUSENAS), 149–50
nationalism, 78–79, 81
natural disaster mitigation. *See* social protection
naturalization, 57, 61, 63. *See also* citizenship
"new normal", 40, 43
New Southern Policy, 71–72
NIC (National Integration Council), 88
night spots, 32
N95 masks, 148
non-contributory benefits, 103–4, 109, 112–17
non-marriages, 14. *See also* marriages

O

older persons
  employment of, 151–52, 157–58
  family structure of, 17, 19, 20, 23
  feminization of, 24, 150, 152
  health status of, 158–59
  with hearing disabilities, 152–56
  population of, 14, 54–55, 61, 64, 150–52, 155–56
  See also capability deprivation
Omicron variant, 40
One Tambon One Product (OTOP) Scheme, 110–11, 115
Oneness Festival, 77
Overseas Investment Firm Industrial Trainee System, 56
overseas travel, 73, 127–28

P

PCA (Periodic Commuting Arrangement), 38–39
PCR (polymerase chain reaction) tests, 40
pensions, 151. *See also* older persons
People's Action Party, 85, 86, 91, 95
Periodic Commuting Arrangement (PCA), 38–39
permanent relocation, 123–24, 127–28. *See also* mobility
permanent residents, 38, 57, 61, 63, 74, 88–91
personal protection equipment (PPE), 149
persons with hearing disabilities. *See* hearing disabilities
physical distancing, 148–49
physical environment, 147, 149, 154–56
physical health risks, 121
polymerase chain reaction (PCR) tests, 40
poor people, 102–5, 107, 109–17. *See also* lower-income persons
population mobility, 121–24, 127–35
population policy (Singapore), 86
post-COVID-19 world, 41–44
poverty
  housing arrangements affected by, 127–32
  during lockdowns, 33
  reduction of (*see* social protection)
  See also economic precarity; hearing disabilities
power imbalances, 103–4, 115. *See also* inequalities
PPE (personal protection equipment), 149
privacy, lack of, 134
property ownership, 35, 37, 42–43, 44n4, 123, 133–35. *See also* housing
psychological wellbeing, 121, 159–61
public housing system, 134–35. *See also* housing
public services, 147, 151
public spaces, 124, 132
purchasing power, 36–37, 123, 129–32

Q

quality of life, 156–62
quarantine, 38–40, 65n3, 121, 133

R

racial inequalities, 35, 38, 93–96
Rajah, Indranee, 85
Rapid Transit System (RTS), 30, 44
Reciprocal Green Lane (RGL), 38–39
recreation, 36. *See also* cross-border commuting
recruitment agents, 53, 59–60, 64
relationships breakdown, 127–29, 136. *See also* family relationships

religious organizations, 74–75
relocation, 123–24, 127–28. *See also* mobility
remarriages, 15–16. *See also* marriages
renovation firms, 33
renting, 130, 134–35. *See also* housing
replacement migration, 88, 93–94
residence, permanent place of, 125, 133. *See also* shelters
residential care facilities, 123. *See also* older persons
resilience building, 102–5, 107, 109–12, 115–17
retirement, 123. *See also* older persons
RGL (Reciprocal Green Lane), 38–39
risk mitigation. *See* social protection
rough sleeping. *See* homelessness
RTS (Rapid Transit System), 30, 44
rural areas, 151, 154–55

S

S Pass (Short-term Employment Pass), 85
salary criteria, 85–86
school systems
  admission policies of, 88–92
  diversity in, 87–88
  foreign students/teachers, 68–69, 72, 80–81, 88–94
  integration efforts in, 93–94
  scholarships offered by, 91–92
  Singapore core in, 95–96
Second Link, 29
Sejong, King, 70, 76, 79. *See also* Korean language
separation of persons, 31–34, 42, 74, 122, 130–35, 144
sex tourism, 36, 44n6
sexual violence, 41, 57, 62. *See also* violence
shared common spaces, 87

shared language connection, 77–79, 81
shelters, 124–25, 131–32. *See also* accommodation
Short-term Employment Pass (S Pass), 85
sign language, 148–49, 160. *See also* hearing disabilities
Singapore
  Central Provident Fund (CPF), 130, 137n1
  "Circuit Breaker", 31, 122, 124
  citizens of, 38, 86, 88–92, 122–23
  Education Ministry, 87–89, 91–93
  Housing Development Board (HDB), 134, 138n2
  housing insecurity in, 32–33, 123, 127–35
  manpower policy of, 33, 85–86
  Mass Rapid Transit (MRT), 33, 44n2
  People's Action Party, 85, 86, 91, 95
  school systems (*see* school systems)
  "Singaporean core", 85–86, 95–96
Singapore-Malaysia connection
  commuting along (*see* cross-border commuting)
  in post-COVID-19 world, 41–44
  ties between citizens of, 31–38, 42–43
single (unmarried) people, 14
skills training, 103, 115. *See also* training
Sleman (Indonesia), 149
smartphones, 161–62
social cohesion, 86, 87, 122. *See also* integration into society
social connections, 127–29, 136. *See also* family relationships
social distancing, 148–49
social housing, 123, 127, 130, 133–35. *See also* housing

social infrastructure, 147, 151
social norms, 147–48
social protection
　during COVID-19 pandemic, 112–17
　and disaster risks, 109–12
　in Thailand, 105–9
　types of, 102–5
social stigma, 148. *See also* hearing aids
social support, 74–75, 127–29
social visit pass, 133–34
sojourning, 60–63. *See also* migration
South Korea
　age structure of, 54–55
　employment system in, 56–57
　foreign policy of, 71–72
　multiculturalism in, 68–73
　migrating to, 51–54, 57–62, 78
　support for migrants in, 69–70, 71, 74–81
Southeast Asian studies, 72
Statistics Indonesia, 145, 150
students, 68–69, 72, 80–81, 88–94
suicides, 33, 41. *See also* deaths
support
　from civil society, 74–75
　from family, 17, 24, 127–29
　for foreigners, 69–70, 71, 74–81
　from government, 75–77, 91–92, 112–17, 121
　for humanity, 102–5, 107, 109–17
surgical masks, 148
SUSENAS (National Social and Economic Survey), 149–50

T
teachers, 92–93, 95–96
temporary shelters, 124–25, 131–32. *See also* accommodation
tensions, 86–87, 93–96. *See also* integration into society
testing for COVID-19, 40, 65n3, 121, 133
Thailand
　age structure of, 54–55
　disaster risk management in, 109–12
　government support during COVID-19 pandemic, 112–17
　migrating out of, 51–54, 57–62, 80
　social protection schemes in, 105–9
training
　in area studies, 72
　in languages, 73, 75–81
　for skills and development, 56, 103, 115
transborder ties, 31–38, 42–43. *See also* cross-border commuting
transient housing arrangements. *See* homelessness
translocality, 34–38, 41–42, 121–24, 127–35. *See also* immigration; migration
transnational marriages. *See* foreign marriages
transnationalism, 52–53, 124–25
travel
　to overseas, 73, 127–28
　patterns of, 121–23, 127–35, 131
　restrictions, 31, 32, 38–39, 121, 133
　short-term (*see* cross-border commuting)
Tuas Second Link, 29
tuition grants, 91–92

U
undocumented workers, 58–63, 69
unemployment, 115, 124, 130, 131, 133. *See also* employment
universities, 91–92
urban areas, 151, 154–55

Index

V
vacations, 36–37. *See also* cross-border commuting
vaccinations, 39–40, 65n3
Vietnam
  age structure of, 54–55
  multiculturalism in, 68–72
  migrating out of, 51–54, 57–62, 80
  support for migrants in, 69–70, 71, 74–81
violence, 41, 57, 62, 75
visas, 57, 62, 69, 131–33
voice attenuation, 148–49. *See also* hearing aids

vulnerable groups, 102–5, 107, 109–17, 127–35. *See also* older persons

W
wage disparity, 52, 57–58, 64. *See also* economic inequalities
women, 24, 150, 152
Wonogiri (Indonesia), 149
Woodlands Causeway, 29
work permits, 31–34, 37–38, 43, 57. *See also* employment
World Bank, 104